This copy of *Sales Crumbs from the Master's Table*

is presented to:

_____

I believe in your gifts and talents and stand in agreement for your *complete success* - Mentally, Spiritually, Socially, Physically, and Financially.

By:

_____

Praise for Sales Crumbs...

"Just finished Crumbs from the Masters Table...excellent, superb and contagious. A great book for our future giants who decide to invest in 20 lunches at the Master's Table. Every sales professional should have this book in their library."
  - Wilfred Holder, Managing Director, Trinidad Insurance Centre Ltd

"Read the entire piece of work and it is excellent! From Lesson one "Crumbs from the Master's Table" to "Yes, LeRoy, I believe it." A great way to leave a legacy of love and learning. It is simple, real and makes very interesting reading. Read the first chapter at my Monday morning meeting and everyone wants to know where they can get a copy! Great Stuff!"
  - Maxim Marquez, Agency Manager, Pan American Life

"I have read dozens of books on sales, but none has been as engaging, arresting and as practical as this edition. I expect that it will be written in several languages so as not to deprive the rest of the world of sales people from the benefit of this work of art, this oxygen in the science, art and profession that is sales."
  -Raymond Tim Kee, Exe. Chairman, Investments & Insurance Services Ltd.

"As usual you do not fail to surprise. The last crumb was a great ending and full of emotion on one simple page. Great work by Brandon and yourself. I felt as though I was in the book...it is a must read for all who know you and those in the sales business either manager or salesperson."
  -Amado Marcano, Branch Manager, Guardian Life of the Caribbean Ltd.

"First, thanks a million times over for "Crumbs from the Master's Table". This book reads like it was written specially for me... I love it and am enjoying the experience. I can only hope that other

persons who read it will get at least half of what I'm getting from it
..."

-Colin Cholmondeley

"I would like to congratulate you and your son-in-law on a fantastic piece. I read it cover to cover without putting it down...It was gripping, educational, inspirational and surprisingly emotional."

-Stuart Franco, Vice President Sales, TSL

"The first in a series of gems is out...Believe me when I say that I could not put it down...There were so many great nuggets to feed off... continued great health and strength to continue to produce more gems to edify our noble industry."

-Ralph Coutain, Branch Manager, Sagicor Life, Inc.

"This book is in the top 5 books I have ever read. It is magnificent, inspiring, uplifting, and rejuvenating..."

-Keith Paul, Chairman and CEO, Keinan Financial & Trade Services Ltd.

"I took my time to thoroughly savior and enjoy every lesson, it is a must read for every seasoned agent and rookie. I like the easy style with which the learning is communicated making it simple for someone to replicate into their own practice. You continue to clear paths for all agents to follow, and it is my sincere wish that agent far and wide will read your seminal work."

-Lennox Barrow, Insurance & Financial Services Limited

"Read the book and I am impressed. It's a template for the new agent. Great stuff!"

-Nathanial William Wilshire, Branch Manager, Guardian Life

"I have reviewed Crumbs from the Master's Table, and it is a masterpiece. It is clearly expressed, well written, superbly structured, and gives scores of precious golden nuggets to brighten understanding of the sales process. It is my belief that in generations to come, this seminal work will become a classic in similar terms to: <u>As A Man Thinketh</u>; <u>The Greatest Salesman in the World</u>; and <u>How To Win Friends and Influence People</u>. Keep strong, and continue the precious journey."

-Philip Guy Rochford, HBM., Author & Life Empowerment Coach

Brandon Clay Enterprises, LLC

THE SALES CRUMBS TRILOGY
VOLUME I

Sales Crumbs from the Master's Table

A Guide to Achieving Sales Success & Life Mastery

Inspired by the Sales Genius of
Conrod Athelstan LeRoy Shuffler

Brandon L. Clay

Published by Brandon Clay Enterprises, LLC
McDonough, GA
www.brandonlclay.com

Copyright © 2012 Brandon L. Clay
Createspace
ISBN-13: 978-1479290772
ISBN-10: 1479290777

Distributed by Brandon Clay Enterprises, LLC.

For ordering information or special discounts for bulk purchases, please email Brandon Clay Enterprises, LLC at orders@brandonlclay.com

Design and composition by Brandon Clay Enterprises, LLC
Cover Design by Brandon Clay Enterprises, LLC

2nd Edition
First Edition Printed February 2011

This work and *everything* I do is dedicated to my best friend and wife, Natalie. All my love and devotion!

To the millions of people, worldwide, who are pursuing greatness that may happen upon one of my works: I believe in the nobility of sales and your ability to be a top professional. My greatest desire is that something said within these pages will impact your life and set you on course to unleash all the greatness that is within you!

I wish you Money, Power, and Success!

Table of Contents

Introduction by LeRoy Shuffler

As the first installment in the fantastic **Sales Crumbs Trilogy**, Brandon Clay's <u>Sales Crumbs from the Master's Table</u> is a masterpiece, an *instant classic*. To have been identified as the inspiration behind Volume I of this Trilogy is one of the greatest tributes ever paid to me. I am much honored and especially blessed to have him as a son (in-law) and as a loving member of our family team.

Brandon is a proven professional, and a master in the art and skill of effective communication. In his unique story-telling style, the reader is spellbound with the simplicity in which the technical points of the sales process are easily explained *and understood*. Excellence is his only standard, and Brandon has hit the target once again.

After more than 50 years of being blessed to be in the noblest profession in the world, I am thrilled to see "Selling and Cultivating" has at long last been captured as a way of life. The **Sales Crumbs Trilogy** is a sales training manual and self-help series skillfully wrapped up in one. I highly recommend this entire work of art as a must read for <u>anyone</u> pursuing selling as a *life* - Rookies, Professionals, and Sales Coaches alike.

Here's wishing you "Success to the Point of Significance".

Conrod Athelstan LeRoy Shuffler

Author's Preface

Pareto Must Die!

For most, sales is daunting, intimidating, scary

Economy is struggling, consumers are wary

Companies hire, on their products they train

Separate the wheat from chaff for a cycle of revenue gain

Set the 80% there, apart from the twenty

Top to bottom success is rare, excuses a plenty

The 20% are elevated, celebrated, we raise our glasses

The 80%, struggle, exit stage right, lost in masses

But from the mailroom to boardroom there is a knowing

That the winds of *change* are fast blowing...

A realization that sales is a profession of nobility

That the members of our teams represent a wide spectrum of ability

That if our organizations are to succeed...reach the next high

Developing all people is a core need...*Pareto Must Die!*

I wrote the Sales Crumbs Trilogy for the 80%. To the newbie in need of confidence, the steady majority in need of guidance to the next level, the wounded warrior in need of revival, the seasoned veteran in need of refreshing, to the manager/coach/mentor in need of tools to help their diverse teams succeed. Some of the 80% are struggling to make their quota, to make ends meet...*to keep their jobs.* The process used to monitor, measure, and motivate them into higher performance is one of "carrots and sticks" (*do this or get this!*) or "sticks and stones" (publically branded with the "Scarlet Letter" of an underperformer).

While it is my staunch belief that "Pareto Must Die", I understand that there will always be some form of "*the minority seling the majority*" that prevails within sales organizations. The real problem is that we **accept it** as a foregone conclusion and then *fully expect* that 20% of our teams will sell 80%. Rather than rage against the Pareto machine, many sales organizations become "sausage grinders". They increase the odds of company success by **recruiting broadly**...*developing narrowly*. This leaves the 80% with no effective guidance or individual development. This has systematically created the collateral damage of high turnover, burn-out victims, and "round peg in square hole" sales people. Ironically, there are **many** in the 80% that are on the brink of breakout success...only needing one more ingredient to make it through to the next level *Sadly, most will never get that ingredient*. I wrote the Sales Crumbs Trilogy for them...*the 80%.*

Be clear, I am not disparaging the 20%, in fact, *I celebrate them!* **I am one of them and have been my entire sales career**. This elite groups of people have worked hard, and have honed their natural (and developed) skills into the coveted role of top producer and income earner. *However, the 20% don't need focused development...just give them to right tools and get out of the way!* More validating; many of them have read *this work* and have given it their seal of approval. *Why?* - because it contains the same concepts that have helped them achieve on the highest level.

While I am called to the 80%, I understand that if members of this group are lazy or satisfied that my energy will be wasted. *Nevertheless, I believe most of the 80% want to get better.* I also understand that regardless of focused development on the 80%, it is mathematically unlikely that sales will spread evenly throughout a dynamic sales organization. **That is not my goal.** My goal is to create more "solid citizens" who contribute to the best of their developed ability, increasing the quality of their lives and building stronger sales organizations!

"A voice crying out in the wilderness." Many times in my career this is how I have felt. Trying to relay the necessity of dealing with the "person *within* the salesperson" was lost on many hard-driving corporate executives who understandably only had profit (and loss) in mind. Unable to comprehend my holistic approach to the *entire person*, they labeled me as an incurable optimist, a player's coach, and a philosopher. *Fortunately, these labels are reflective of who I am.* Thankfully, I have been given several opportunities to engage my contrarian approach to sales development. The aforementioned attributes may not normally be credited to sales leaders, but they are the essence of the values I used to create great success for 5 start-up organizations. My most recent assignment was a fledgling healthcare company *with zero membership*. Within 12 months, it became the fastest growing and eventually the largest of its kind. That same company was sold to the largest healthcare company in the U.S. That success has afforded me the opportunity to pursue my passion - **Helping millions achieve success...*one at a time*.**

Based on my experiences, I realized the need was great for an *evolved* approach to coaching personal development in sales. I wrote the <u>Sales Crumbs Trilogy</u> as a series of progressive stories that will take the reader on an **inspirational and instructional** journey to achieve a higher level of sales *and* life excellence. They take the reader from *struggle to success* through the life of Matthew "Matt" Palmer. Matt is a universally relatable character who finds himself in a world that he knows nothing about - sales - *but desperately needs success in it.* The concept of "Sales Crumbs" is designed to symbolize bite-sized, easily digested lessons. Simple, yet profound truths relayed in an engaging "page-turning" format. The chapters are intentionally small and each contains a central learning and several revelatory peripheral lessons - *<u>all the while entertaining, empowering and enlightening.</u>*

I wrote the <u>Sales Crumb Trilogy</u> to reaffirm the core elements of time-tested sales professionalism - Integrity, Sincerity and a Desire to Serve - while providing <u>excellent product solutions</u>. It is time to revisit the venerable principles that were the foundation of the oldest profession in the world (*no, not that one!*) - *Sales!* It is time to allow each individual to use their own authentic "sales voice". Developing this voice will provide *first nature confidence* and not <u>second nature training</u> that requires force of will to execute.

Certainly, there are core elements of sales that are scientific, but there is the art of sales that is born out of individuality that should not be pigeon-holed, categorized, or suppressed through rote scripting. The trilogy outlines the "science of sales" but appreciates the idiosyncratic nature of the "art of sales" and creates an avenue, through an engaging parable, for the reader to discover *their voice*. I have been in the profession of sales for 28 years and seen it from all perspectives. I have been fortunate that each progressive opportunity has allowed me to grow and develop *my voice* - a uniquely authentic voice that has transcended industry and economy.

In 2011, I was inspired to write the first volume of the trilogy - **Sales Crumbs from the Master's Table**. I distributed several thousand copies to sale professionals and leaders from all walks of life, various countries and industries as a "pilot". The reaction to this initial title was overwhelming and confirming. That title was art imitating life. As I committed the ideas of a modern day sales parable to paper, a voice continually spoke to me from the blank pages. It was the voice of Conrod Athelstan Leroy Shuffler. As a proud man of Guyanese descent, he speaks the King's English but yet has a distinct Caribbean flavor. I, on the other hand, have a "sing song" southern drawl - albeit one peppered with words of collegiate academia. In many ways, our lives are a study in contrast, but there are two things that bring us together; his beautiful daughter, my wife Natalie...*and the love of* *sales.* Volume I is fashioned after LeRoy, considered a living legend by many of his disciples. *It is art imitating life.*

LeRoy is truly a sales professional and professionalism is the core skill of selling that *never* changes...he is sales personified. Don't allow the simplicity of the concepts to dissuade you, <u>at the core of every great professional selling transaction is a great relationship</u>. While I have taken some poetic license in writing this book, the core concepts are LeRoy's real world wisdom of over 50 years of perfecting his craft. I have also injected my sales experience into these pages and much of it is autobiographical. The combination is a potent mix of the art of relationships with the science of selling and presented in an uncomplicated, yet impactful way so the lessons resonate in your professional and personal lives.

So if you are new to selling, or if you are a seasoned sales professional, this book is written for you. It will connect you to, or remind you of what is great about the profession of selling, help you cultivate more lifelong relationships and generate more personal satisfaction - which ultimately, will lead to more income! *It will help you become a professional seller - the noblest of all the professions you could engage in.* I believe this series of books can be a vital component of your journey and as is my custom, **I wish you Money, Power, and Success!**

And now, Volume I of the Sales Crumbs Trilogy...

Near death of a salesman

Matt is already sitting up at the edge of the bed when the alarm clock goes off at 6:00am. His wife, Erin, rolls over and rubs his back, "Good morning honey, were you up all night again?"

"Yes, just couldn't fall to sleep," he said groggily, "A cup of your good coffee and I will be fine for the day." He leaned over to kiss her and rub her belly.

"Let me make you some eggs and toast to go with that coffee," she said lovingly. She was always very attentive to Matt, even though her life was busy, too.

"No, for now just the coffee...I am not real hungry. I am going to take a shower to get ready for work," he relayed with a hint of melancholy.

Work - that word had now taken on a whole new meaning. As he showered he began to play over in his mind the events of the last 3 months. He was laid off from a well-paying salaried position as an analyst at a prominent financial institution after only one year of employment. Despite all the networking and posting of resumes on every conceivable website, the global economic meltdown had taken all the demand for what he did out of the job market. As they were living solely on saving and Erin's income, he answered an ad for Financial Services Sales - Consumer Insurance Division. He had all the licenses from his old job and while he had never sold before, the Human Resources manager said they would train him. Truth be told, Matt took this sales job as a last resort, hoping that he could do this a few months until analyst opportunities emerged again. The pressure was on as this new position paid a small salary for 3 months, and then he would be on commission only. He knew something had to give, but this was his best...no, his *only* option right now.

He entered the kitchen to see his wife putting some food on the table. She had been so supportive of him through the first two years of their marriage. They met as freshmen at Fulbright College where Matt received his Finance degree and Erin, an Education degree. They were inseparable the four years of college and married life was good. Their first baby was due in 3 months, so she had gone from full-time to working part-time as a teacher at the local elementary school. Financially, things were ok, but tightening with each passing day. He did his best to hide his anxiety, but she could see right through him, but she never seemed to dwell on their circumstances. She was his biggest cheerleader and never let on if she was worried, too.

"Coffee ready?" he asked.

"Yes, sweetie, but I still made you something to eat. You can't work all day on an empty stomach."

As he struggled his way through the eggs, he began to dread the day that was ahead. It was Thursday, and he and 20 other new recruits had just completed 5 days of orientation and 3 days of product training. Today was the first day on the phones trying to secure new clients. He was mortified at the prospect of cold calling...even though the sales manager told him these were warm contacts. Supposedly, they were orphaned clients that had not been touched in years but had bought a policy, or they shown recent interest. Regardless, they didn't seem "warm" to him.

Then, there were the weekly Monday sales meetings where the production and activity for the previous week was put on public display. Though he had only attended two of these meetings, he quickly discerned them to be a kind of peer pressure motivation. All of this sales stuff was new to Matt, and because he was smart, he had been able to fake his way through these first 8 days. *That was short-lived.* Today was do or die and he was scared.

Erin hugged and kissed him and told him to have a great day and that she believed in him. He felt like a kindergartener who was being pushed out of the house for his first day of school. The world seemed big and cold, but he knew he had to make this work. Once he got to the office, the sales manager showed all the new recruits to a series of tables, each with 4 phones. The sales manager began his canned speech for the new team:

"As newbies, you have to work your way up to a cubical, then a shared office, and for the superstars, a private office with an assistant. I will provide you a list of warm leads daily, and at the end of each day, you will bring them back to me with your activity sheets. These sheets will be used to post your activity for the Monday sales meetings and will be reviewed by me and the sales director weekly. *Remember, the phone is your friend!* Ladies and gentlemen, start your engines!"

For the first time, Matt wished the normally long-winded sales manager would talk longer. He inevitably made it to Matt's table and gave him and the 3 other newbies sitting next to him, their daily "gruel with a crust of bread" leads. He knew his moment of reckoning had arrived. The day was a blur, he didn't know what he was doing, and had absolutely no confidence. The sales manager walked around like a drill sergeant and told several of them they were squandering the precious leads provided. Matt felt lost and with each unsuccessful phone call, a bit of his soul died. Thus went Thursday...*and Friday.*

Monday came much too soon, which meant the weekly sales meeting. There was ruckus applause and cheers for the new recruits who actually convinced some of these warm leads to meet with them. Amazingly to Matt, they had appointments to pitch the products that week. There was even more riotous applause for the top guns - the top producers that were selling like crazy. Their numbers on the board looked like a fantasy football league. It represented everyone from six-figure superstars, a rumored 7-figure giant, to those struggling to stay afloat. Matt wondered inwardly, what the top producers were doing, and more importantly, how he could do it, too.

After the meeting, the sales director pulled Matt and 5 other newbies into his office to tell them that they were already behind the other recruits and that the next 30 days were critical if they wanted to remain with the company. Matt had *never* been called out so publically, and prided himself on being excellent in all that he did - a work ethic instilled in him by his father. His embarrassment to be included in the underperforming category quickly turned into pressure.

Desperate for direction, he approached his sales manager for help. He was empathetic, but told him that he has his own quota and 10 other recruits assigned to him. "Take the pitch book, and products guide and study them this week," was all he could offer as if Matt had not already poured over them gaining no magical insight.

He then got up the nerve to approach the top gun, Larry Wilcox, who was the rumored 7-figure earner, to see what fast advice or assistance he could offer. Larry hazed him as a "newbie" and quickly dismissed him like he had the plague. Not rudely, just resolutely as someone who didn't have time for amateurs.

Finally, he notices the old man who always greets everyone each sales meeting with a warm smile and hearty handshake. He was always well dressed and carried under his arm a leather portfolio. That was it - no smartphone, laptop, office, personal assistant, or even a cube. Matt had met him the first day of orientation but could not remember his name.

"Who is that man?" Matt asked pointing to the old man.

"Him? We all refer to him as the dinosaur," Larry quipped.

"*His name is LeRoy,*" interjected Larry's personal assistant. "From what I hear, he has been with the company for over 30 years," she continued. "He is friendly enough but a *little odd.* Every Monday morning meeting he shakes the hands of everyone and greets them with a 'Happy Monday' and wishes them 'Great Success' when they leave. Seems as though the company just tolerates him because the President loves him and he must have been somebody *ages ago.* Strange, but his name is not even on the sales leader board. I guess he is a lonely old man with nowhere else to go so he comes here."

Matt works up the courage to approach him. He was anxious for help from anyone and LeRoy had certainly been with the company long enough to know *something* that could help him.

"Good morning LeRoy," Matt began nervously.

"Happy Monday to you, it is a fabulous morning," LeRoy said enthusiastically.

"My name is Matthew Palmer, but please call me Matt. I am one of the new recruits."

"Yes, I know. How is it going?"

"Still trying to get my feet wet."

"Well, there is water everywhere my friend, jump in and join the rest of us for a good swim," LeRoy said with a big smile.

"That is just it...I don't know how to and I was wondering if you could teach me how to swim in the sales world?" said Matt relieved that he had gotten the request out so quickly.

"*Why me?*"

"Because I hear you are one of the best," trying his best to mask being incredulous.

LeRoy puts his hands on Matt's shoulders and draws closer. "Here is a *free* lesson. Never say anything you don't believe to be true, that is genuine and from the heart. Clients will be able to detect you are disingenuous and you will repel them quickly. *So I take it that you have already gone to your sales manager?*"

"Yes. He says he is too busy," Matt replies with his head down.

"Of course he is too busy. He has his own quota and many other new recruits. What about the people on top of the leader board, they would be a more obvious choice? Like Larry Wilcox, perhaps."

Matt relays he did that already and he dismissed him and called him a sorry rookie.

"Understandable, as you have not yet demonstrated a worthiness to be mentored. *Larry has no time to waste.* Then I suppose that makes me, an old man with time on his hands, your *last resort?*" LeRoy sounding vexed.

"No...I mean, yes. Look, the sales director said I was already behind the other recruits and that I had 30 days to prove myself. I have been unemployed the last 90 days, and my base salary runs out in less than 3 months. I am expecting my first child, my wife is working part-time and I am essentially living on savings. I pride myself on working hard and delivering great results, but in less than two weeks of being here, I have already been warned about losing this job. *So yes, I am desperate.* Yes, I can use your help...no, I *need* your help." Matt felt the emotional weight of the past 3 months and two weeks pour out with each word.

LeRoy pauses a moment, "Thank you for sharing your situation with honesty. Honesty is pure, it is the seed of integrity, and will compel people to your vision and aide...for these reasons, *I will help you.*"

Matt is relieved, even though he isn't even sure LeRoy knows anything that can help him. Just the thought that someone would reach out to give him a hand provided a momentary mental reprieve.

Leroy continues, "I will take you under my wing and tutelage for the next 30 days, *but my wisdom will cost you.* The price is 20 days of lunch at your expense. I always go to the local corner cafe. I have been going there for over 30 years, and I always get the daily special for variety. It is very tasty and filling and as you know, a man should never work on an empty stomach!"

"I just explained my financial situation and how the salary runs out soon. I don't see how I can afford to do that in the position I am in," Matt says objecting to the terms.

"I am being economical by enjoying the lunch special which is $7.99 plus I leave a 20% tip for a total of $10 a day. The terms are quite reasonable," LeRoy counters.

"That will be 20 lunches times $10 - $200 for the month!"

"*Here is your 2ⁿᵈ free lesson.* If you are not prepared to invest in your education for success then you will *never* achieve any," LeRoy says in his trademark venerable style.

"I won't be able to eat."

"Perfect! You should be listening anyway. *So you agree to my auspicious terms for a month of enlightenment?*" asked LeRoy executing a text-book assumptive close.

Matt could only think that all the old man wanted was a free lunch, or someone to talk to. But in his current position, he really didn't have much choice. He was between a rock and a hard place so he capitulated.

"Agreed," Matt said hesitantly. "*When do we begin?*"

"Today of course...I am hungry!" LeRoy answered with the satisfaction of a master salesman who had triumphantly won a new client. With a handshake and a smile from LeRoy, they headed over to the cafe.

Monday - Lunch #1 Crumbs from the Master's Table

As they entered the cafe, it is obvious that the owner and the staff all knew LeRoy. He smiles at each of them warmly and gives them his customary "Happy Monday" greeting. They all seem genuinely happy to see him, even though he has been going there for years. He takes Matt over to introduce him to the owner.

"Today is a special day," began LeRoy. "Allow me to introduce Matthew Palmer, a new advisor with our company. He and I will be enjoying lunch together at your wonderful establishment for the next 30 days."

"Welcome Mr. Matthew," said the owner, "You are in the company of a great man. Moreover, he eats everything I bring him and always seems to enjoy it as though it was his last meal. I presume you would like today's special Mr. LeRoy?"

"As customary, but my friend here will not be partaking. He is in class and I am the instructor," LeRoy said with just a hint of gloating.

"He could find none better, for truly, you are supremely gifted in that area. Wonderful. Mr. LeRoy, can I interest you both in bread?" asked the cafe owner.

LeRoy replied as if this was a play that was staged, "You can always interest me in bread - warm with butter, please!"

They were seated just on the outer edge of the cafe, almost outside, where they were close to the sidewalk and could see all the people coming in and out of shops and businesses on the street. The bread arrived and LeRoy bowed his head briefly in prayer, then immediately begins tearing the warm bread and slathering it with the butter. A couple of bites and the oversized crusty roll was gone. Matt noticed that two birds had just flown in and were coming close to the outside table. He was preparing to shoo them away when LeRoy stopped him, "Hold on a moment, these are my friends and *my* invited guests."

He takes the butter knife and skillfully collects a pile of bread crumbs and slides it off the edge of the table into his hand. *The two birds come boldly forward and eat right out of his palm!* He then places a portion of the crumbs on the ground right next to his well polished shoe. The birds continue to enjoy their bounty which brings a big smile to LeRoy's face. Matt was amazed and perplexed. *Had he gotten involved with some crazy bird man?*

LeRoy reflects for a moment, looking off into the pristine blue sky and then says in a deeply reflective manner, "God always takes care of his little ones, even if it is just Crumbs from the Master's Table. It has been proven to me throughout my life and of this I have no doubt. Tell me Matt, *do you believe that?*"

He is not sure what to say. He remembers that the old man seems to have a sixth sense that can discern whether he is telling the truth. So he says honestly, "I would like to believe it, as I could surely use some help myself right now."

"Here is Lesson #1, and this *is* paid advice. Since you are just starting out, don't chase the big deals. Go after the crumbs - the little accounts, orphan accounts, the type of accounts that the top guns feel don't warrant their time. *Don't despise small beginnings as they will lead you to greater things.* You need a series of experiences and starting small is the best way. To continue the metaphor, *simply go after the crumbs.*" LeRoy turned his attention back to the growing crowd of little birds, who were still enjoying their meal.

"As my little friends here have demonstrated, while you were ready to shoo them away as a nuisance, I was ready to embrace them and give them what they needed and desired. My reward is a *trusted relationship.*" He then turned to look right into Matt's eyes, who remembered the sting he felt being dismissed by his sales manager, and then Larry when he asked for help just an hour earlier.

LeRoy continued his impassioned speech, "Start small and give the best service you can provide for where you are in the moment. I know there are many things you do not know yet, but good character and a willingness to serve will see you through to the next level. People who are not used to being served in this manner are more grateful, loyal, and will trust you enough to take the good things you have to offer - despite your current lack of experience. They will remain lifetime relationships and as raving fans, they will tell others about you. *Just look over at the curb at my raving fans.*"

There were at least 10 other birds who seemed to witness what LeRoy had done for the two birds. He then throws the rest of the crumbs their way, which they enjoy.

"That alone is worth 20 lunches and is what created the man you see before you today," he said as he took a few sips of water. Matt could tell he was fighting back a well spring of emotion as the words flowed from a deep spiritual place. Whatever LeRoy knew seemed to bring him great daily joy and more importantly, *peace.* At that moment, that is the one thing he would have paid 1 million lunches for. As if by the power of osmosis, the same feeling came over Matt and for the first time in a several months, he felt...*hopeful.*

LeRoy finished his lunch and Matt was about to flag down the waiter for the bill. LeRoy stops him and says, "No need, just lay a $10 bill on the table and we are good to go!" He waves goodbye to the owner and gives a rousing "Stay Powerful" as he turned left to go wherever he goes each day. Matt turns right to go back to the office. It was time for an afternoon of calling on warm leads, but this time, *with a renewed feeling of faith.*

Tuesday - Lunch #2 Why are you here? *Part one*

The next day, Matt was walking over to the cafe for his daily meeting. Apparently, LeRoy only goes into the office for the Monday morning meetings and Tuesday through Friday he visits with his clients. Matt surmised that work had become more of a social activity for him. He had asked around and found out LeRoy was in his late-sixties and had come to this country over 30 years ago from Guyana in South America. That would explain his dialogue - his diction was immaculate, but Matt could detect a Caribbean accent. No one had a bad thing to say about him and to all of them he was the gregarious, kind-hearted, albeit eccentric enigma. LeRoy must have gotten to the cafe early and the same scene from the day before was playing out, down to the spontaneous but almost scripted banter between LeRoy and the cafe staff, the warm bread and butter...and *yes, the two birds.*

LeRoy immediately asks Matt to open his notebook. "Please write at the very top of the page in big letters the question, <u>Why Are You Here?</u> Take a moment to think about it before you answer as this is the most important question you can ask and answer," he says, like a taskmaster.

"I am here because I need money," Matt answered with a 'duh- like' sarcastic tone.

"We all need money but there are hundreds of ways to make it. Again, I ask...*why are you here?*"

"Because I lost my job in the financial services industry, couldn't find a comparable position, and I answered this ad and they gave me this job." Now Matt was getting agitated at the question.

LeRoy sensing his frustration, elaborated, "Ok, I can see that you are lacking the proper motivation to make a go of this business. Everything you have said thus far is about fear, about pressure, about necessity and about your circumstances. For a moment, think of me as a genie in the lamp...with a Caribbean accent! *What do you want out of life?*"

"I want to be able to pay my bills and take care of my family."

"That is noble and do-able. After you have taken care of the basics, *what then?*" LeRoy was pressing for him to think deeper and more expansively.

"I would love to buy my wife a beautiful new home to raise our children," he answered perking up a bit.

"Ahhh, the American Dream," replied LeRoy. "It is the dream of all humans to take care of those they love. But for a moment, go wild. What crazy things would you want if there were no limitations?"

"I would love for the home to be in a golf community as I would love to play golf on the weekends. I want to have nice cars," Matt said warming up to the exercise.

"Continue, what kind of cars?"

"A nice family sedan and a Porsche 911 for weekend excursions..." He began to run down a list like a child on Santa's knees and continued, "I would love to help my parents so my dad could stop working so hard, and I want to have nice clothes, watches, like the top producers have."

LeRoy interjected like a carnival barker, "*And how would having the ability to live like that feel?*"

"It would be amazing, liberating and satisfying!" he exclaimed.

Leroy was silent for a few moments as he could tell Matt was in the throes of imagining these things as possible. He understood that these brief but focused visualizations were powerful and could help break the myopic view of *current* needs that had engulfed the young man.

"The first thing you must do in life is determine <u>*what*</u> <u>you want</u> and <u>*why*</u> <u>you want it</u>. These two together will create a white heat of desire and that motivation will spur you to action...even in the face of obstacles, rejection, temporary failure and self-doubt." He continued, "You must determine what you want in *every* area of life -mentally, physically, socially, spiritually, and yes, financially. You must determine why these goals are important and allow the *carrot to rule more than the stick*. You must design a life that will compel you, support you and become your seeds of ambition and accomplishment. I like to call this Archimedic Leverage."

"Isn't Archimedes the guy that said 'Give me a lever and a fulcrum to place it on and I will move the world'?" Matt remembering an abstract lesson from college.

"Eureka, a scholar indeed! The lever is made up of <u>what you want</u>, the counter weight is <u>why you want it</u>, and the <u>how becomes the fulcrum</u> - *able to bear the full weight of your wildest imaginings.*"

"I can see it now. The emotion of *why* will offset my doubts and fears and make everything feel possible," said an enlightened Matt.

"I am thrilled you understand! One of the greatest lessons you can comprehend is that <u>How Hard You Try Is Based On Why</u>. One last time Matt...*Why Are You Here?*"

Matt now realized that the question was less about why he was here at the company, and more about why he was here on this earth. It was about his goals, dreams and aspirations, which would help him see beyond his current needs and circumstances. It was all the wish lists of life that he and Erin would lay in bed talking about for hours - they had not talked that way in quite a while as he was preoccupied with his current condition. LeRoy was directing him to who he wanted to be and his impact to mankind *beyond himself.* The notion of crafting a bigger meaning excited him and troubled him all at once. He had never thought of his life quite this way before, *but he knew it was time.*

Wednesday - Lunch #3 Why are you here?
Part two

It was now the third day at the cafe and the same scene from the previous days plays out. Matt felt like it was the Twilight Zone, but now *he was in the movie*.

LeRoy breaks the ice, "Did you and your wife speak last night?"

"Yes, we did," Matt replied excitedly.

"How was the conversation?"

"I have to tell you, that it was exciting, hopeful, and then began to overwhelm us as we thought of how can we do this when our current situation is so unstable?"

"That is normal," LeRoy explained, "For once a man gets a powerful vision, the specter of fear <u>must</u> make its appearance. That fear can do one of two things...it can push you back to complacency, or it can motivate you to pursue answers. *Which one is it for you?*"

"I have too much at stake to give up...I have to press forward," Matt said boldly and resolutely.

"Good. Then you have already broken through the thin veil of fear. You must continue to be motivated by the positive images of your goals and dreams."

"But LeRoy, right now, I can't see how- "

"I didn't ask you how, I simply told you to dream," said LeRoy, uncharacteristically cutting him off. "We will begin dealing with *how* straightaway. Let me ask you another question. *Why are you here?"*

"I thought we dealt with that yesterday?" Matt wondering if LeRoy was fighting senility.

"We only looked at it one dimensionally from the angle of what you will get out of the deal. *Today, we must look at it from the client's view."* LeRoy once again instructed him to pull out his notebook. "From the client's point of view...*why are you here?"* he asks.

Trying to be thoughtful, Matt stumbles around the concept of selling products and providing good service and offers, "I am here to provide high quality products, delivered with the highest level of service, honesty, and professionalism."

"Not bad for a high school yearbook entry, but at the end of the day, those are things that the client *expects* - to get a product that meets their needs and done so professionally. That will put you square in the mix of 100's of other professionals that the client has access to. *You need a mission statement.* Use the fewest words possible to convey why you are here for the client."

"I have to tell you, I am stumped. I don't even know my product well and you are asking me to develop a mission statement of what I will do for my clients." Matt was truly baffled, "*If you don't mind me asking, what is yours?"*

"Early in my career, my mission statement was not unlike the one you just espoused. I quickly realized that cliché sounds good as a bumper sticker but was not enough to motivate me or my clients." LeRoy began to reminisce as he recalled his own personal history, "As I began my career chasing the crumbs as we discussed on day one, the amount of rejection I received was incredible and discouraging. I knew these were the people who needed what I had to offer the most, <u>but they were not buying</u>. Through the discouragement, I realized that my mission was wrong. I wanted to sell products, when I should have been *focused on how my products provide solutions to their problems, concerns, hopes, and dreams for the future and that of their family.*"

Matt shook his head in agreement. He followed LeRoy's line of thought, but still needed more help to come up with something. "Ok then, if you are not here to sell products, why are <u>you</u> here?"

"At a critical point of my development, like you, I was a young man, recently married with a child, and another on the way. The financial pressure was building but I did not want to convey my desperate situation to my potential clients. At that time, I heard the great Martin Luther King, Jr. say in a speech":

'The time has come for us to civilize ourselves, by the total, direct, and immediate abolition of poverty.'

He took a moment to reflect on what was obviously a profound moment in his life, "My mission became to Eradicate Poverty."

"That is a lofty goal," said Matt.

"A true mission statement should take you *beyond* your present circumstances into a higher level of possibility and greatness. Yes, a lofty goal, but one that I attempt to manifest *one person at a time*."

LeRoy continued, "To expound, the first person I had to accomplish the eradication of poverty for, *was me*. I realized that poverty was a mindset, a form of mental disease and at that stage of my life, I had all the symptoms...pressure, hopelessness, a lack and scarcity mentality. Before I could ever make a good living with this business, I had to change *my mindset*. I became motivated by my desire for a better life for me and my family...the things you discussed with Erin last night. *I also focused on how I would serve mankind to warrant those financial blessings.* Think of your current situation Matt - how does it make you feel?"

"Sick to my stomach," he admitted with candor.

"As I like to say, poverty is hell! Yes, that is a graphic but accurate description. To Eradicate Poverty has driven me to get up each day and continue on when things looked darkest, but also at a point in my life where all <u>my needs</u> were met. It is not a means to an end *because there is no end*. There are still people that <u>need</u> what I do, and what you do. Do you understand?"

"Yes, I think I do. I need a mission statement that conveys how I want to serve, not only my clients, but mankind?"

"Correct! Think hard about it tonight and tomorrow we begin to make that mission statement come to life." LeRoy actually looked exhausted from the day's discussion. He had spoken with such great conviction it gave Matt a glimpse into what would make this man come to work with great energy and purpose after so many years. Matt began to realize that he was not a dinosaur at all. He was a man that had not yet fulfilled his mission and it would not allow him to rest...*not yet*.

Thursday - Lunch #4 The nobility of sales

A s the ritual of the bread crumbs was proceeding like a well choreographed tango, LeRoy asked Matt what mission statement he had developed for himself.

"Here is what I came up with - *Helping People Build Generational Wealth.* What do you think?" Matt asked timidly hoping for LeRoy's approval.

"It is not important what I think. The relevant question is will this mission statement sustain you through the hard times? Even more importantly, will it provoke you to continued action when you are wildly successful?" LeRoy asked emphatically.

"Yes, it will," Matt retorted proudly.

"Then it is perfect, and yes, *I love it!*" Both men's expressions indicated they knew they had just passed a major milestone. "One last question and don't think me mad. W*hy are you here...from the company perspective?*"

"I am here to market their products in a professional manner and make my quota," Matt answered laughing.

"Give that man a gold star for the right answer, the first time. Quite simply, any company worth working for would expect that you will be an extension of their image and brand and do so in an exemplary fashion. Yes, you are right that they expect value for their investment in you. Even with your paltry base salary, as you put it, they are investing *heavily* in you. Investments of time, energy, and resources and you must provide a return on that investment through revenue generation....*sales*." He leaned in like he was about to give Matt the secret to the universe. "The first thing *you owe* the company is to <u>love</u> the selling profession. Tell me Matt, *do you love it?*"

"I have never done it before, and so far, I have not been very successful, so I can't love it...*right?*" Matt asked looking for a way out of the question.

"Remember you said the first day I met you that you only took this job because you couldn't find another salaried position and that you were forced into sales as a last resort?" LeRoy asked like an investigator of a heinous crime.

"Yes, I remember," he was almost too embarrassed to acknowledge it now - just four days later.

"Unfortunately, your initial negative perception of sales is widely held by many, shamefully, *even* people in the organizations that rely on what we do to sustain *their jobs.* In some organizations, sales teams are viewed as second class citizens, and in the extreme, a necessary evil. While that is counter-intuitive and acutely counter-productive, they have the right to their opinions. However, for you and me, being representatives of this splendid profession, it is reprehensible not to believe in the nobility of sales. *What kind of effort can you give if you don't believe what you are doing is noble and valuable?*"

"I guess you are right," Matt said apologetically.

"I know I am right! Let me explain it plainly. The profession of sales is fundamental to the human experience and critical to *human existence*. That is not an overstatement. Imagine a farmer in Idaho growing potatoes. *Can he live on potatoes alone?* Of course not. He needs clothes, food, electricity, equipment. What is the *one thing* he needs to provide these things for his business and family?"

"Money?" Matt responds with all the confidence of a three year old.

"You didn't need your finance degree to get that one right." says LeRoy almost sounding condescending. "*How does he make his money?*"

"Selling potatoes," he says firmly.

"*Is he doing the actual selling?* If so, is it a roadside stand that only a few people will pass, is it the local farmer's market - perhaps. Or is it a global potatoes exchange where a professional potato broker finds him clients all over the world to buy his produce? Matching his ready supply to the world-wide demand for all good purposes - French fries, baked and loaded, chips, or bio-fuel to run the cars of the future?" LeRoy's cross examination was quite forceful and effective. He finishes strongly, "Will the farmer, a noble profession in its own right, make it without a professional seller?"

"I guess not. I never thought of it that way before," Matt conceded to the pure logic of LeRoy's line of questioning and closing argument.

"The power of professional selling is that in its basic form, it connects a buyer to a seller, a need to a supplier. For that connection and transfer of value, the professional seller is rewarded. <u>Selling connects all humans in one way or another</u>. To understand this connection will give you great pride and power of conviction of the nobility of sales. Do you know how many people work at this company?"

"There are 60 people in our office," Matt had learned in orientation.

"Yes, but that is only our sales branch. In the home office and nationally, there are over 25,000 employees. *How do they make their money?*" LeRoy inquired.

"Their salaries are based on what they do for the company."

"*Where does the revenue for those salaries come from?*" LeRoy grilled driving home a mighty point.

"Our sales!" Matt exclaimed for the first time understanding the value of sales to the corporate collective.

"Correct! From the mail clerk, claims specialist, customer service, all the way to COO and President - **all** of them derive their living from what you and I do. When you call them and tell them you are in sales, they should regard you in the *highest*, not disdain you as the *sales guy*. In reality, they are here because of what we do for our clients."

LeRoy was on a roll, like an evangelist behind a podium dispensing his brand of eternal truths. He pressed on, "In its purest form, professional selling is the highest form of human service - to you, the client, and to the company and its employees.

When you are excellent, the rewards are great and come in three forms;

First is emancipation. *You think a salaried position brings security?* That is false. When your old company let you go, could you easily find another equitable position? Ahh, but if you are a professional seller, matters not what you sell, the world is always looking for you! You are free to choose the next mountain to conquer and no one can deny you the opportunity."

He wiped his brow and the sermon continued, "Second is gratification. When done properly, the profession of selling gives a high sense of accomplishment as you assist people in achieving their desires, or solving their problems."

Matt could tell he was flowing now. LeRoy rolled on, "And thirdly, remuneration. The true sales professional relishes the *unlimited income* potential of selling. With a salary, you get paid for *your time*. Give 40 hours and a company will give you a check. With sales, you get paid for *your results*, and if you do it well, the client you secure today, can pay you for a lifetime through residual income. Ultimately, the fear of living on commission is directly tied to your self-image. To raise your income in sales, you simply need to raise your self-image."

Matt wasn't sure if LeRoy would ever come up for air, but the oration was inspirational and giving him a new perspective on the selling profession. "Shame on the people who try to make us feel guilty about deriving that three-fold satisfaction from our hard work and dedication. Yes, we earn more but that income is proportionate to the value we create. Sadly, the dichotomy of *wealth and worthiness* has many sales people engaging in subliminal self-sabotage. You have to know that you are delivering critical services and not to shirk the rewards of that service. *Matt, you must cut yourself loose from limiting beliefs right here and right now!* Realize that sales is one of the rarest opportunities in life to benefit from one of the greatest universal truths, ordained by the Master himself" -

"As I serve...I deserve"

LeRoy concluded, "Ask me why I am here from the company perspective? *I will tell you because I am a professional seller and sales is a noble profession!!!*" Repeat that 3 times after me...*I am a professional seller and sales is a noble profession!*" LeRoy wasn't taking no for an answer so Matt joined in on the 'call and response' portion of the revival.

While their impromptu pep rally was garnering unwanted attention from the adjacent tables, Matt felt a surge of energy going through his body for the first time since graduating college. He felt good about his goals in life, the service he was going to give, and the value of that service...he felt passion and purpose coursing through his views...*he felt powerful.*

Friday - Lunch #5 The power of chemistry

For the first time, Matt was actually excited about the job and jumped out of bed refreshed and ready for the new day. He was so energized he approached the top gun, Larry Wilcox, and asked him if there were any small accounts he didn't have time for and that he would split any commission 30/70, explaining he needed the experience. The top gun said, "Here is a small fish that wants a face to face meeting next Monday. Have at it and, of course, if you sell him, I get 70% - *deal?*"

"Yes, those are the terms," Matt felt like a wheeler dealer. He remembered the first lesson LeRoy had given him and knew it was time to get in the game even with a small beginning.

"Deal!" said Larry, "Good luck...*you will need it.* With my limited interactions, Mr. Jacobs seems like a mean old bird."

That didn't matter, he was so proud that he had his first real opportunity he couldn't wait to tell LeRoy at lunch. Cordially, he waited for the lunchtime ritual to be completed and said to LeRoy excitedly, "I have my first sales meeting next Monday. *What do you think about that?*"

"I think that is tremendous progress, and your excitement reminds me of my first sale. Unlike you, I was petrified and paralyzed. I did not know my product and I was about to try to convince a total stranger to give me money for something I didn't understand. *Not you.* You are eager and ready."

Matt's demeanor changed drastically. In his new found energy, he forgotten that he didn't understand the products the way he needed to. Yes, he had been given three days training on their product's features but he really didn't know how to *sell them.* He looked up from the table and asked LeRoy tentatively, "*Would you go with me?*"

"That would only make you more nervous as you try to interact with the client the way you think I would want you to. Or worse, you would try to sound *like me...*it will be many years before you are *that* smooth!" LeRoy sensed the agony the young man was facing and asked, "I have never asked about your wife. Tell me some things about Erin."

Matt was more than ready to change the subject, so he shared how they met in college and immediately hit it off after his awkward approach. He talked about how pretty she was, smart and supportive of him in everything he did. He lit up discussing her and it was obvious he was truly in love and considered himself a lucky man.

"May I ask if she is perfect? Don't worry, she is not here and I promise not to tell!" LeRoy said with a wry smile.

"No, I guess not. No one's *perfect.*"

"*No?* Can you think of things you would change about her?"

"Nothing that matters," Matt was a little perplexed and perturbed.

LeRoy continued unfazed, "So, let me understand a few things, she is not perfect, you have things you would change, and you married her anyway...*right?*"

Matt, not fully realizing where this was going said, "Yes, of course, and I would do it all over again," he stated defensively.

"*Would she say you were perfect?*"

"Uhhh...let me think...*NO!*"

"So there are things she would change?" LeRoy asked.

"Yes, of course!"

"But she married you *anyway*, in spite of your lack of perfection and things she might change about you?" said LeRoy with a smile of satisfaction noting Matt's glimmer of enlightenment.

LeRoy then said very profoundly, "There is no perfect product, no perfect sales person, or perfect client. No product will ever be 100% of what a client needs, but it must meet their major wants, needs or desires. *What makes them come together in this environment of imperfection?* I am glad you asked...*Chemistry!*

As you described Erin's features, you spoke with conviction, passion, and honesty. Do exactly that with the features of your product until you become an expert. In the meantime, that infectious energy will compel a potential client to listen and then make a qualified decision about buying from you.

If there are important things you don't know about your product...tell them you will find out and get back with them."

He paused to give his statements a chance to marinate in Matt's mind. With a nod of understanding LeRoy explained, "Chemistry is not about manipulation, or pulling the wool over someone's eyes. It is about creating an avenue where the imperfect salesperson (you), can take an imperfect product, but one that meets the major needs of their client and consummate a sale. *Does that make sense?*"

"Yes, it does," Matt answered as he recalled that many of his friends had told him he had no chance with Erin at Fulbright College when they were freshmen. She was the popular, beautiful and brilliant girl that was "out of his league". He had built up the nerve to approach her out of a dare with friends and while awkward, that forced meeting turned into a night of dancing, talking, and *instant chemistry*.

LeRoy broke him out of his trance, "Do you feel better about next Monday?"

"Actually, and *strangely*...yes."

Monday - Lunch #6 The intimacy of sales

The morning's sales meeting was a good one for Matt. He actually had a face to face meeting to report! While he was still somewhat uncomfortable having his results on public display, at least now he had a "1" on the board! A few congratulatory back slaps from his manager, a couple of new recruits, and Matt was back to the phones.

At lunch, LeRoy was even more jovial than normal. He kept saying 'A beautiful day!' and 'Happy Monday!' to all who passed. Matt asked, "Why do you wish everyone a Happy Monday?"

"Monday is the first day of a new work week," he began. "It signifies the ushering in of new opportunities and possibilities. Most people dread Mondays - from calling in sick in order to extend the weekend, to the statistical prevalence of heart attacks - Monday *has an undeserved bad rap.* I see it as a day of renewal, much like New Year's Day. We should cheer it and celebrate it! Happy Monday! *Speaking of weekends…how was yours?*"

"It was great! Erin and I did more talking and planning about our future, my mission, and the upcoming meeting next Monday."

"*How was the sex?*" LeRoy asked most casually.

"Pardon me?" he said incredulously. "Did you just ask- ?"

"*Yes, how was the sex?*" LeRoy repeated. "I assume with all the positive discussion that the two of you were intimate?"

"NONE OF YOUR BUSINESS!" Matt exclaimed looking around to make sure others had not overheard the inappropriate question.

"Exactly, it is *absolutely* none of my business. Even with the chemistry you and I have established the last week, you are not comfortable sharing every intimate detail with me...*are you?*"

Matt was relieved that at least he understood that they weren't *that close*, but he also understood LeRoy usually had a line of reasoning for all his off the wall metaphors and analogies.

"Ok, now that you have my undivided attention, what is the correlation?" he asked.

LeRoy jumped back in, "Your clients will be the same. Just because there is chemistry, buyers don't want to disclose all the intimate details of what they need, desire or what they enjoy. They don't want to express that they can't afford something or expose past mistakes they have made when making buying decisions."

"But aren't those things that I would need to know?" Matt had fully calmed down and was ready to extract the lesson from the shock of the moment.

"How do you get to intimacy in marriage? Please pardon my graphic illustrations, but in many respects, sales are a result of an intimate relationship. Let me explain. It requires foreplay. *You should not be in a hurry to demonstrate what your product can do to solve a need that you haven't even uncovered yet.* You must determine what they need, want and desire and then gain agreement to proceed. That is done through communication. You must focus on meeting their needs. You cannot serve your client while being fixated on your commission, the next prospect, or hurrying up the proceedings. As humans, we all have different approaches to decision making and you must allow for these differences with patience and understanding. *Does any of this sound familiar based on your relationship with Erin?*"

Matt had to admit the logic, though he had never once thought of these dynamics of human interaction in the sales process. He thought that someone simply *needed something* and found someone who could provide it. This was more complex, but logical. He finally answered, "Yes, it sounds like Valentine's Day last year," not believing he just said that to a man LeRoy's age. *He didn't even talk like this to his father.*

Unfazed and amazingly comfortable with all the double entendres, LeRoy continued the analogy, "A true sales professional is there *after* the sale is consummated. This is actually more important than all of the things leading up to the sale. You want to express thanks, check in with them to be sure all is well with the product and that they are satisfied. Then and only then, can you expect additional business from them, and referrals."

While the metaphors made Matt more than a little uncomfortable, he understood what LeRoy was trying to say.

"Again, pardon the graphic nature of today's lesson, but as a married man of over 50 years and 8 children, there are some things you cannot take for granted in relationships and selling is just another type of relationship. I think that is all that is needed for today's lesson," he said wiping his brow finally showing signs of discomfort. "Please leave the $10 bill and I will see you tomorrow."

Tuesday - Lunch #7 What scares you? *Fear of failure*

LeRoy seemed eager to begin the lesson today. He reviewed the last week of lessons saying, "We have spent the first several days looking at what this opportunity means to you, the client, and the company. Would you agree that there is great potential and likelihood that *everyone will win?*"

"Yes, I can see that now," Matt said with a fully renewed mind about the profession of sales.

"How does that make you feel?"

"Optimistic and encouraged about the future."

"Great! Now, a very important question, *what scares you?*"

"What do you mean?" Matt asked not grasping the full intent of the question.

"What do you think will keep you from attaining the level of success and contributions we have established over the last week? It *will* be some form of fear manifesting itself as a barrier. So I ask again...*what scares you?*"

"While I feel better than I did my first day, my greatest fear is still failure," he relayed not believing he had allowed himself to say the words.

"Good! *That is what it should be?*" LeRoy responded matter-of-factly.

"*Good?* How can fear of failure be good?"

"Fear as a paralyzing agent is *never good*," LeRoy explained, "But fear that mandates external investigation and personal introspection will always lead you to a stronger plan to overcome challenges and barriers to success, *thus destroying failure*. What would constitute failure to you?"

"Not being able to take care of my family by succeeding in my mission to help families build generational wealth," Matt offered knowing instinctively to connect his vision to his mission.

"I congratulate you.   At least you connected your personal situation to your mission statement. The two should be inextricably woven together so that the need for answers is mandated.   Let me ask a question - is someone buying our product right now...this *very moment*?"

"Yes, I guess they are."

"More specifically, is there a newbie and/or a veteran producer selling our product this very moment?"

"Yes, without a doubt," as Matt keeps an interested eye on the daily sales leaderboard.

"*Is that new rookie or veteran better than you?*" LeRoy asked in a challenging voice.

"No! I mean, I don't know...they are there selling...and I am here with you. *No offense.*"

"None taken," LeRoy pressed on, "Then your fear isn't whether people <u>will buy</u> or <u>are buying</u> our product...the real fear is whether they will buy it *from you*?"

"Yes, I guess you are right," he owned up.

"Then, this isn't about the product or clients, the *real fear* is about you, right?"

"Right?" he admitted sheepishly.

"Easy!"

"*Easy?*"

"Yes, if people weren't buying *anything from anybody, then everybody would fail.* Conversely, if people *are buying*, they are buying from *somebody*...right?"

"Right!" Matt declared triumphantly understanding that *someone* was going to be successful regardless of circumstances or economic environments.

"Then, in the words of Rev. Jesse Jackson, you have to become that somebody."

"I hate to state the obvious, but isn't that why I am buying you lunch everyday....*so I can become that somebody?*" said Matt trying not to offend LeRoy's sensibilities but drive home the intent of their daily meetings.

"You are closer than you think, and yes, you will get your money's worth from these sessions," he remarked feigning aggravation. "I saw golf clubs in your car...*do you play?*"

"Of course!" said Matt reacting in a defensive tone.

"To clarify, just having clubs in your car does not mean you play. *You do have unused sales kits in your car.*"

"Touché," Matt conceded, "That makes us even on smart-alecky remarks!"

"Are you any good?" LeRoy asks unfazed.

Matt explains, "It is not that simple. In golf, it is not a matter of whether a player is good or not. I have a handicap that allows me to play people of other abilities so we can compete fairly."

"Please explain that to me," demonstrating his obvious lack of golf knowledge.

"I am a 6 handicap. Knowing that would allow me to play with someone that has a 22 handicap and at the end of the round determine who played the best based on their established handicap index and the course difficulty. While it sounds complex it creates a level playing field."

"What are the playing differences between someone with a 6 handicap from someone with a 22?" asks LeRoy probing for details.

Talking about golf, Matt lit up with excitement, "A 6 handicap will likely be 250+ yards off the tee compared to 225 yard drives for a 22 handicap. I will reach the green with my next shot giving me a chance for a birdie putt. The 22 handicap golfer will take up to three shots to get to the green and will be taking their first putt for par if they are lucky, but most likely for bogey. As a 6 handicap, I will make my fair share of birdies, but mostly pars and only an occasional bogey."

"Then, in a word, what separates you as a 6 handicap from someone with a 22 handicap *is skill?*" LeRoy asks with a new understanding.

"Yes, that would be fair," Matt said trying to remain modest.

"How did you develop this skill?"

"In a word, *practice*," Matt said as he began to see Leroy's point.

"*Were you good the first day you went out?*"

"No, in fact I was nervous because I didn't want to embarrass myself in front of my 3 buddies I was playing with," recalling a particular outing.

"How do you perform when you are nervous?"

"Not so good. In fact, I whiffed my first tee shot. I started to sweat like a pig. Thankfully, it was summer so no one could tell," Matt said laughing.

"Whiffed?" LeRoy asked not understanding the golf jargon.

"It means I set up to hit my tee shot, waggled a couple of times pretending to knew what I was doing, and then took a mighty swing at the ball - only to look down to see the ball was still sitting peacefully on the tee...*whiffed!*"

"What did you do after the round?"

"I had a couple of drinks with the boys and then went to the driving range to practice tee shots."

"Did you whiff any then?"

"Yes, plenty of them," Matt divulged.

"Was it embarrassing?"

"No," he admitted.

"*No?* Just a few hours earlier you were, in your own words, sweating like a pig from a whiffed tee shot. *Why weren't you embarrassed then?*" LeRoy again driving home a profound point based on a real life situation.

"Because I was, aahhh...practicing," revelation hitting him hard.

"So if practicing is *safe*, what should you spend most of your time doing?"

"Practicing," Matt said enthusiastically.

"*Practice will expose areas that need development in an environment of safety. Performing will expose those same deficiencies in an environment of embarrassment.* A few more questions - how long was it before you became proficient in driving off the tee?"

"I practiced all I could, almost every day in good weather and even in my dorm room as I studied. I held a club and visualized hitting the ball. All in all, it was about 3 months I guess. In about 1 ½ years I was a single digit handicap and now 4 years playing, I am a 6?"

"Are there people who have been playing longer than you that aren't as good as a 6 handicap?" LeRoy asked already knowing the obvious response.

"Yes," Matt answered.

"So time *alone* is not a determining factor of if someone becomes a good golfer. *It is a combination natural talent, intense practice, visualization and a passion for excellence.*"

"Yes, when you put it that way," Matt acknowledged. He never noticed the practice component of golf because it was a love for him and the time passed quickly when he engaged in the activity.

"You must be willing to dedicate that same approach to the profession of selling. <u>Your first core fear is one of competence and confidence</u>. Those can be overcome with dedication. That dedication will turn into skill developed through experience. Does that make sense," LeRoy knowing that Matt had followed him each step of the way

"It makes perfect sense - with golf, you are talking my language!" said Matt building the correlation and knowing what it would take to develop the necessary skill to build competence and confidence.

"Then you *have* gotten your money's worth...so enough for today."

Wednesday - Lunch # 8 What scares you?
Fear of rejection

I t was an overcast Wednesday, but that didn't stop LeRoy from saying it was a beautiful day. He genuinely seemed oblivious to any form of negativity or bio-rhythmic ups and downs. It didn't take him long to get into teacher mode. He began, "Let's talk about the second greatest fear in the profession of selling after fear of failure. What, young Matt, do you think it is?"

Matt had actually spent a good deal of time on the phone the day before analyzing his call reluctance, so he was positive he had the answer. "It is the fear of rejection," he said knowingly.

"Yes, that is it exactly."

"Do you still have fear of rejection?"

"While I am rejected daily in various strata of life, I no longer fear it, nor am I fazed by it?" LeRoy shared as he took a bite of his food.

"How did you get over it?" Matt asked knowing this was his current stumbling block.

"The way we all do. - I moved on to the *next* opportunity. I kept moving forward and doing that until I realized to <u>never</u> take rejection personally."

"I have to tell you, it does feel personal," Matt lamented.

"I recall when I first came to this county. I had been a great sales professional in Guyana so I had that experience to draw from. I was confident because of previous successes, but the culture shock was too great for me...*and America*. I found myself selling Tupperware®-*like* products in high rise office buildings." LeRoy made that admission and for the first time, he seemed a little embarrassed.

Matt couldn't help but dig a bit, "Tupperware in high rise office buildings, pardon me...Tupperware-*like* products in high rise office buildings?" he mocked.

"Yes, I did not have a car so I had to go where there was a concentration of people. I could see 100's of people in a week as compared to my colleagues in residential neighborhoods that could only see dozens," trying to sound logical to recover his dignity.

"How did you do?"

"As you could imagine, I faced rejection, ridicule and in some buildings security officers who escorted me out of the building. Of course, this was before No Solicitation signs."

"But of course, you are above reproach!" quipped Matt.

"Being the mid-seventies and with my strong accent, I was rejected more than I had ever felt in my own country. I began to develop the approach avoidance that afflicts many sales people and I began to doubt my abilities," he confessed with the pain showing on his face reliving the difficult time.

"*So that feeling is normal?* I have begun to hate the phone so you are talking right up my alley," Matt said empathetically.

"Yes, approach avoidance is normal, and even understandable, but is very dangerous to the psyche of the salesman. I began to think I had made the wrong decision to bring my wife and 8 children to this land of opportunity. One day, I happened into an office building occupied by a fellow Guyanese businessman. Of course, we hit it off instantly, and he even called all 50 of his employees into the lobby where I pitched my products...*the results will amaze you!*"

"Everyone bought from you, *right?*"

"Not exactly. In fact, quite the opposite - *no one bought!* In fact, a couple of them said it was sad to see a proud Guyanese professional selling Tupperware-*like* products," laughed LeRoy at the absurdity of his circumstances and the profundity of that day.

"I bet you were devastated!" said Matt thoughtfully.

"Devastated indeed! Certainly, I am a man of flesh and blood - I was greatly vexed. Angry at *my* people, *my* countrymen and *myself* for being in that situation to begin with. I was a winner and I knew it! On the walk home I had an epiphany. I realized that rejection comes in all forms - sometimes prejudice, sometimes ignorance. It can manifest as the buyer's fear or simply their inability to afford my product. Sometimes rejection is about timing, which determines client receptivity - the right product presented at the wrong time results in rejection. There are occasions when the client doesn't acknowledge or understand how my product can meet their needs or desires. What I realized most by being totally rejected by my fellow countrymen is NEVER MAKE REJECTION PERSONAL!"

"What did you do?" Matt asked interestingly. "Stop selling Tupperware-*like* products?"

"*Are you kidding me?* No, after my epiphany, I began selling it like mad!" he said proudly. "*I evolved my approach.* I began going into the high rise cafes where people congregated for lunch. When people had leftovers, I gave them sample products to pack them in to take home. They could then bring back for lunch the next day. I told them that they could save money by preparing food at home, or bringing in their leftover dinners and using the newly popular microwave. I gave them samples on Mondays through Thursdays and only asked for orders on Friday, which was payday for most of them. In less than 90 days, I was the top cultivator for the company," he relayed as if it was his proudest moment.

LeRoy continued with a great sense of satisfaction and accomplishment, "The same high rises that I was escorted out of, I fondly became known as the Tupperware man! I supported my family of 8 on that job and my strongest memory and learning was about rejection, and the law of averages."

"Ok, law of averages?" Matt asked knowing he was opening Pandora's Box.

"You laughed when I said that I went to business high rises to sell my product. Yes, while my number of rejections was higher, *my opportunities were higher also.* Let's say that I saw 100 people a day and had a 3% close rate. How many would I sell in a day?"

"That's easy...3."

"What about my colleague that went door-knocking in middle class neighborhoods who saw 20 people a day. What would his close rate have to be to sell the same 3 people?"

"15%," said the finance major.

"That was five times my close rate," said LeRoy.

"But you made the same income, right?"

"Yes, even though my rejection rate was 5 times his, we earned the same professional income. But once my <u>skill</u> increased and my close rate increased to 6%, how many would I sell?"

"You would sell 6 people a day, twice the number of the neighborhood salesman?"

"Yes and twice the income!"

Matt had his own epiphany, "I get it! The only way to increase professional income is to either see *more* people, or *more effectively* close the people you see...*or even better, do both*!"

"Excellent observation! The law of averages is scientific and mathematical. You said yesterday that people are buying products from *somebody*, right? If you operate the law of averages and control your fear of rejection -"

"Eventually, I will be the '*somebody*' they buy from and I will be successful!!!" Matt said victoriously.

"Quite assuredly, you will be successful indeed," LeRoy affirmed. "Understand, to <u>see</u> more people requires *more* effort, *more* determination, and *more* rejection resistant grit - s*imply, more effort.* To <u>close</u> more effectively *requires more skill.* As we alluded to in the golf skill development discussion, that skill comes from confidence and competence, which comes from experience."

"The more experiences I have, the faster I learn and evolve and develop skill," Matt echoed. "That takes me back to our first lesson. I shouldn't despise small beginnings but endeavor to have as many experiences as possible."

"Beautifully expressed - for anyone new to any industry or position, they must be prepared *first* for the Effort Phase. The Effort Phase is the process of seeing more people and having as many experiences as possible in the shortest time possible. This combination of getting started, moving and to keep moving will bring many *perceived failure eperiences.* But it will also bring some successes. The successes will eventually come more often and you will break through the Effort Phase. This is commonly known as paying your dues."

"There is no doubt I feel like I am paying my dues," Matt said now feeling like he belonged to a fraternity. "How do I know if I am doing enough to break through?"

"If you are *doing something about doing something,* then you are on the right track. Each phone call should be a little less intimidating, each rejection should not be life ending. You don't want to be callous or oblivious, you *simply move on.* That is why it is important to know *why you are here* so that you can pay your dues with an eye on the bigger picture - your goals and your purpose.

At the point where you move on naturally, the law of averages will deliver you from the process with regimented precision. Eventually, you will move into the Skill Phase. *But you must first conquer your fears.* Once you do that, the things you desire for yourself and others will be inevitable."

Thursday - Lunch #9 Hero worship - *Who is your role model?*

Thursday afternoon was another beautiful day and Matt and LeRoy were sitting in their usual spot when Matt asked, "What is the lesson for the day?"

"Eager I see, but that is good," said LeRoy. "A Buddhist proverb says 'when the student is ready, the teacher makes his appearance'... and here I am! I am humbled and honored to pass on my experiences." They both share a good laugh and Matt opened his notebook to capture key learnings.

"Let me ask you, when you were a child, who were your heroes?"

"Wow! That takes me back. Like any kid, I had lots of them. Oh, now that I think about it, I was about 7 years old and I loved the Mighty Morphin Power Rangers®!" he said excitedly.

"Who was your favorite Ranger?" LeRoy mildly familiar with the show from his grandchildren.

"That's easy…it was Tommy. At first, he was the Green Ranger, then he became the White Ranger and finally, the White Ninja Ranger."

"*Why was he your favorite?*" LeRoy asked.

"Because he was the leader and the coolest. I remember after watching the show, several of the neighborhood kids would get together and act like them. I would wear Tommy's color and slick my hair back and we would throw karate and ninja moves till dark. Looking back on it that was the most fun I had in my childhood! I remember on Halloween, I begged my father for a real White Ninja outfit and he got it for me! I remember being so excited and proud because I was a *real* Power Ranger!"

He had begun to relive his childhood fantasies with such vivid imaginings and recollections, that he had a child like grin on his face.

LeRoy asked him, "Did they ever inspire you to take karate?"

"I wanted to, but my dad said we couldn't afford it."

"Did that stop you from pretending?"

"No way! We really thought we *knew* what we were doing and looked good doing it!"

"All from emulating your heroes?" LeRoy added now pushing to make his point.

"Yes," Matt replied.

"Let's do the same thing for you as a sales professional. Let's pick a role model in this area. *Who would you most want to emulate in our company?*"

"This month's top producer, of course!" Matt said confidently.

"Tell me why?" asked LeRoy probing for him to go deeper with his selection.

"Because he makes the most money, gets great recognition, and he drives an expensive sedan *and* sports car. I also hear that he has a fabulous house at the country club on the lake."

"I would suggest to you that while this month's top producer is certainly a high income earner, let's take a look at how he secures that income," LeRoy interjected. "Did you notice his mix of new sales versus repeat business and referrals?"

"No, I just saw the total production," Matt admitted knowing the other shoe was about to drop.

"Exactly! I noticed that 80% of his business comes from new sales, 10% repeat business and 10% referral. *What does that mean to you?*"

"He is predominately selling a lot of new business. *Isn't that a good thing?*"

"Of course it is. Did you notice who #3 was?"

"Yes, I did. It was Larry Wilcox and he was only *slightly* behind the #1 & #2 producers."

"Good observation. Let me tell you that Larry is exactly *opposite* of the month's top producer in *how* he gets his business. He received 30% of his business from repeat clients, 60% from referrals and only 10% from new business. I happen to know that Larry just purchased a Porsche 911, he lives in the same exclusive neighborhood and actually makes *more* annual income than this month's #1 producer."

"How is that possible?" inquired Matt.

"Was this month's #1 agent, also #1 *last month?*"

"Not according to the leaderboard," Matt kept an interested eye on the rolling reports.

"But was Larry still in the top 5?" asked LeRoy.

"Yes."

"Tomorrow, annualize Larry's total production and you will see for the year, he is #1 with a bullet. That is because he is *consistently* in the top 5. Understand, for motivation of the troops, the monthly activity gets the most attention with parking spaces, plaques and applause, but it is Larry's stamina and staying power that is rewarded in ways that don't get the full monthly fanfare. He will get *that* at the end of the year...which he has done two years in a row...and this will undoubtedly be his third."

Matt began to understand that the monthly ranking, while good, was not the sole indicator of who would be best to emulate.

LeRoy offered, "In review of *how* they get their business, which of them do you think works *hardest?*"

"The agent that was #1 this month because most of his sales were from new clients, and new business requires more energy, *right?*"

"Exactly! Let's create a distinction in the way we can go about getting business and building income. *One way is as a producer, the other is as a cultivator.* The producer concentrates on new business which requires each day he has to "start over" and work to build a new relationship from scratch. Larry, as a cultivator has business *meeting him* at his desk - repeat business and referrals...each day...*who would you rather be?*"

"When you put it that way...Larry Wilcox," said Matt.

"Make no mistake, we must all be producers in the Effort Phase of our career, and my statements are not meant to disparage the current months #1 producer. He is likely in the Effort Phase and paying his dues, *successfully I might add.* Larry is deep in the Skill Phase where business comes to him and that is more sustainable over the long haul."

"What is the key to becoming a cultivator?" Matt asked with great interest.

"<u>The key is turning new business clients into raving fans who will see you as a trusted advisor and only buy relevant products from you</u>. They will refer everyone they know *to you.* If the #1 producer operates with a high level of integrity and provides superior value to his clients, he will be a cultivator with more repeat business and referrals...*in due time.*"

"What if he doesn't?" asked Matt instinctively knowing the consequences.

"Then he will be cyclically up and down the leaderboard. He will expend great energy generating selling opportunities. Eventually, producers will burn out, while a cultivator has energy to spare because they spend most of their time presenting solutions to a ready, trusting audience versus trying to find someone to pitch. *Does that make sense?*"

"Yes, I understand fully and I want to be a cultivator!"

"Then you must model the behaviors of a cultivator. We will begin that tomorrow. For now, it is time for me to have lunch."

Friday - Lunch #10 Excellence - *The only standard*

Happy Friday! "This is our last meeting before your big appointment on Monday. *Do you feel ready?*" asked LeRoy.

"I feel better than I did last Friday, but I must admit I am very nervous," Matt replied.

"Let's deal with that today. Tell me why you are nervous?"

"I don't know the client and I heard he can be difficult and I am still learning the product," Matt divulged.

"Tell me, which of these two things can you control, *the product or the client?*" asked LeRoy looking to pin him down to the source of his apprehension.

"Neither?" he asked hesitantly.

"Affirmative! You cannot control your client or your product but you can control you! Never prejudge the client and know that the product is already a pre-defined component of the process. That being the case, *what should you spend most of your time on?*"

"Myself...*right?*"

"Exactly. In many ways <u>you are the product</u>." LeRoy expounded on the point, "Let's examine the important characteristics of the professional seller; *appearance, demeanor, enthusiasm, confidence, communication, compassion, integrity, and knowledge.*

Certainly, there are more, but these reflect the *outward areas* that are most noticeable to the client. Please note, that knowledge is *intentionally* last. You may have heard this saying before;

'They do not care how much you know until they know how much you care!'

"While very cliché, it is very accurate from the clients' point of view," said LeRoy finishing the thought.

"That seems like a lot of characteristics to be," Matt responded.

"You are correct sir! The real key to that lengthy list of attributes is not *to do them* but *to be them*! Being is the highest form of excellence and excellence is the only standard! Realize that excellence is not a matter of chance, *but a matter of choice*. Just like you work on your golf game, you must work on yourself and develop and refine the traits necessary to *BE Excellent!*

Matt was almost at the point of being overwhelmed, when LeRoy gave him additional comfort about his appointment on Monday. He asserted, "To *Be Excellent*, you have to *Be Yourself*. Of all the traits of excellence, the ones that are most important *shouldn't* require development - they are integrity and compassion. These are characteristics I know you have in over abundance. Exhibit these, be yourself and good things will happen. *I guarantee it!* How do you feel now?"

"I am still nervous, but ready like Freddy."

"*Who is Freddy?* No matter, I believe you are ready!"

Monday - Lunch #11 Abort mission!

Another sleepless night, but this time it was more from the excitement of having an actual sales meeting, than his normal tossing and turning adventure. Matt readied himself, putting on his best suit and his lucky tie. Erin attended to him as usual. She hugged and kissed him, called him her hero and off he went for a day that he felt would change things forever. Even the morning sales meeting was different as Matt was recognized for having his first client meeting. A round of applause and a few pats on the back made him feel special. *Just wait until he comes back with the sale!*

He walks up to LeRoy just as he is leaving, "Since I will be missing lunch today, I have already been to the cafe and paid in advance for your special today."

"Organizational skills and keeping your commitments are true signs of a future sales leader," said LeRoy reaffirming his considerate gesture.

"Wish me luck," said Matt wishing secretly that LeRoy would accompany him.

"Godspeed," he says all of a sudden a man of few words. Matt knew that it was too late for him to dispense some groundbreaking truth and that he had to walk this out on his own.

He felt like he was going on some type of field trip, but he was a man on a mission. While he was nervous, he knew that Mr. Jacobs needed what he had to offer, *so it should be easy.* As he turned left unto what was supposed to be the street where Mr. Jacobs lived, he panicked when the name was different. He kept going straight, hoping that he would run into the right street, but he didn't. It was now 9:55am and the appointment was at 10am. As he continued to retrace his directions, he realized he made a wrong turn a couple of miles back. He tried to contain the anxiety and the sweat that was now running down his face, wiping frequently. At 10:10am he arrived at Mr. Jacobs home. *That's not too bad* he thought, ringing the doorbell.

"You are late!" bellowed Mr. Jacobs blocking Matt from entering his home.

"Yes sir, I am sorry, I got turned around and took a wrong turn," Matt said apologetically.

"You have to be more respectful of people's time. I almost left you high and dry. *What is this all about anyway?*" barked Mr. Jacobs obviously agitated.

At this point, Matt knew things had to change and in a hurry, so he jumped right into his pitch, "Mr. Jacobs, our records indicate that you are currently underinsured and that you need additional protection to ensure your family will continue in the lifestyle you have created after your death -"

"Death! *Is that what you are here for...to sell me life insurance?*" he shouted.

"Well, yes...I mean, there are other things too," Matt now sweating profusely from getting lost, standing on the steps in the sun and now the grilling he was getting from Mr. Jacobs.

"Son, you have just wasted my time and yours, *and late to boot!* I ain't interested in buying life insurance...good day!" The door closed, not with a slam, but with a gentle click of the lock with Mr. Jacobs on the other side.

Matt stood there motionless for a few moments, reeling from the thrashing he had just taken. *What just happened? Is this what the sales "profession" would be like? What would he tell Erin, his sales manager and director...what would he tell LeRoy?* For now, he just wanted to go home. Then he realized he had to go back to the office - the phone was still waiting on him and it was going to be a long afternoon.

Tuesday - Lunch #12 What does the client want?

A s Matt turned the corner to the cafe, LeRoy, the cafe owner and the entire staff could read how Matt's appointment had gone the day before. It was written in his countenance, his walk - his entire demeanor. They all tried to act as if it was a regular day, but they all knew he was disappointed.

"How did you sleep last night?" asked LeRoy breaking the awkward silence.

"Not very good. I tossed and turned reliving the disaster of yesterday's meeting. I suppose you must have guessed it didn't go very well," he answered dejected.

"Let me ask, *did you learn anything?*" LeRoy asked firmly.

"*Yes...I learned that selling is tough.* I learned that getting people to understand they need what you have is a difficult proposition...should I go on?" Matt relayed in a whiny tone.

"Learning is never disastrous, particularly if you don't repeat the things that you perceive went awry. *What was your key learning?*" LeRoy seemed determined to make him live the painful moments again.

"I don't know because so much went wrong."

"Were you yourself and did you convey honesty and integrity?"

"I didn't get that far. Once I told him that I was there to sell him life insurance -"

LeRoy interrupted him abruptly and somewhat harshly, "No wonder it went so bad, *who in their right mind wants to buy life insurance?*" He called the cafe owner to the table and asked him, "Do you want to buy life insurance?"

"I think not," started the cafe owner, "I am going to live forever!"

"Do you see any insurance salesman in here today?" LeRoy asked.

The cafe owner pretended to look high and low and responded, "I only see one, but since he is with you, *he is okay*," he said snidely.

Matt didn't think any of this was funny and turned to the cafe owner, "Ok, so if I am an insurance salesman, what does LeRoy do for a living?" thinking he finally caught LeRoy in his own trap.

"*What does Mr. LeRoy do for a living?* He Eradicates Poverty. I thought everyone that knows *him*, knew *that*! Where have *you* been the last two weeks?" said the cafe owner walking off to get bread.

Then it hit Matt like a ton of bricks, he had gone in and forgotten his mission of helping people build generational wealth and had reduced himself to a simple salesman. "Now I understand," he said contritely, "Never forget the mission and let that drive my motivation."

"Wonderful learning! As we noted early on, your mission must sustain you in tough times and when you are wildly successful. Never forget the mission!"

As Matt settled down LeRoy told him, "These next three sessions will focus on *the client* as that is the next element you must perfect. The lessons will be brief but vital to you becoming a true sales professional. Regarding yesterday and clients in general, *what does the client want?*"

"My mind is still reeling. I guess the same things that would be important to me - my family: their security and happiness," Matt supposed.

"Very good, as that is a critical list. *In summary, they want solutions to their problems and fulfillment of their desires.* Which of these things does our product do?"

"That depends as our products can solve a problem *or* fulfill a desire," Matt answered.

"Great answer. *Who determines which it is?* Whether our product solves a problem or fulfills a desire?"

"The client?" asked Matt with diminished self-belief.

"Let me ask it another way. When you tell your clients that your mission for them is to Help Them Build Generation Wealth... *which* of the two will you be doing?"

"Depends on how the client views it. It depends on what they want or need in the moment," Matt answered slowly building his mental strength.

"Perfect answer, as it could be *both*...solving a problem or helping fulfill a desire. Your mission statement is constructed in such a way that *the client* determines which one is vital and what it would mean to them...*even before they tell you explicitly*. Never lose sight of the fact that you are there to serve the client and the needs and desires of their lives. That will serve you well going forward. If that is the key learning from your meeting yesterday then you will be *infinitely better* the next time."

"I hope so," Matt says and then he sees the disapproving look in LeRoy's face and corrects himself, "I mean, I *know* so!" Real success is built on a series of learnings that come from apparent failure. *You have not failed - you cannot fail.* You are still learning so don't fight or begrudge the process of gaining experience. Take it from an old man...you will be fine *in due season*. We will take it from here tomorrow."

The words resonated in Matt's mind and he instinctively knew LeRoy was right.

Wednesday - Lunch #13 What the client doesn't want

For the first time in the two weeks of meetings, it was raining outside. The cafe owner had pulled in the plastic cover to keep rain from coming in on the patrons. LeRoy was in his usual jovial mood, but *things seemed different.* He realized that the normal patter with the cafe owner and the staff over the requesting of warm bread with butter had been forgone today. Wondering what might be wrong Matt asked LeRoy, "*What, no bread today?*"

"On days when I can't feed my friends, *I don't partake.* It is a subtle reminder that enjoyment comes from having someone to share your blessings with. It also confirms that as the birds will surely show up tomorrow, that God took care of them some other way today."

Matt was starting to truly understand the motivation of this man, who had poured so much wisdom into his life in such a short period of time.

LeRoy began the second lesson of the day, "Yesterday we talked about what your clients want - *answers for their needs and desires.* Conversely, we have to review what the client *doesn't* want. *What might that be?*"

"I am not sure."

"Think of your own experiences with buying a product," prompted LeRoy to get him to think deeper.

"I don't like pushy sales people!" Matt exclaimed.

"What does *pushy* mean?"

"They are so fixated on *selling me* that they don't wait to find out what I want or need before they jump into their pitch," he replied.

"So they were *'Selling by Telling'*?" LeRoy asks rhetorically.

"Yeah! A perfect characterization!"

"So like you, your potential client doesn't want to be <u>told</u> <u>or sold</u>...would you agree?"

"Yes, that is right on."

"Oddly and somewhat counter intuitively, the *worst* question a sale person can ask is 'Can I help you?'. On the surface, it seems like an innocent question, but what do you normally say when asked this question?"

"My knee jerk answer is always 'No, thank you'," as he recalls a recent store encounter buying a suit in a department store.

"Please understand that your statement is more a *reaction than a response*. On the rare occasion that you say 'yes', it is because you only need a clerk and *not* a sales professional. *That reduces the sale to a commodity.* One based on price and availability, not a process."

"Yes, just show me where it is and what is the price, nothing more," added Matt fully understanding the principle from his suit buying experience. He had trouble finding the size of a suit he wanted and only engaged the sales person to check the back for his size.

"That is ok when you are selling a candy bar, but will never work when you have a complex sale or expensive product. It will not work when you want to build repeat business, referrals and life-long relationships...*if you want to be a cultivator.* Clients want to be heard and understood. My father always told me, '*You have two ears and one mouth...use them proportionately*'," he declared. "Clients want to be enlightened."

"I agree and understand. *They don't want to be told or sold, they want to be served!* "

"I feel like you just snatched the marble out of my hand young grasshopper!" said LeRoy satisfied that the young man grasped the essence of the lesson he was trying to impart.

Even with the sting of his first meeting with Mr. Jacobs still fresh, Matt was beginning to feel like he understood what he needed to do. The pieces of the puzzle were starting to come together.

Thursday - Lunch #14 What does the client know that you don't?

Another beautiful day and the sun was shining brightly. Just as LeRoy had predicted, his little friends re-emerged from the previous day's showers. Right on cue, the little ones politely requested their daily bread, and LeRoy was more than happy to oblige them. He began, "Today's question will sound odd but will provide great revelation in how to proceed to convert a prospect into a client." Matt was now intrigued and felt today was going to close the gap between him and his prospective clients.

"Don't keep me in suspense...what is it?"

"*What does the client know that you don't know?*" he asked.

Matt felt stumped and LeRoy was waiting as if the Final Jeopardy® music was playing in the background. "There are <u>three key things</u> that the client knows that you don't...*what* they need or desire, *why* they need or desire it and *when* they will buy it. If you knew these things going in, how much easier would your job be?"

"Infinitely easier!" Matt replied.

"Do you think that Mr. Jacobs will eventually buy financial or insurance products?"

"Yes, he will," he said confidently.

"*When* will he buy them?"

"When he realizes he *needs* them."

"Correct! We have a saying in the insurance business - the client wants to buy insurance the day *before* they need it...and not a moment sooner! Of course, this sets them up for potential catastrophe when unforeseen events occur. From our topic yesterday, does a client like Mr. Jacobs want to be told he needs life insurance and that he needs to buy it?"

"No. He was very proud and more than a little stubborn," Matt recalled. "Oddly, he is the one that requested the visit so he must have had *something* in mind...*something* he needed. Of course, I didn't get far enough to determine *what* that was."

"Mr. Jacobs was certainly proud, but stubborn...maybe not," said LeRoy. "To your point, he obviously wants something but has not had the *right* enlightenment to facilitate a sale. As we discussed yesterday, he rejected your *'selling by telling'* and being asked *'may I help you?'*. So his reaction, not a response, mind you, only makes him *appear* stubborn. The key to professional selling is getting the client to verbalize these things so you can provide the proper enlightenment. *How do you get them to share these three key items with you?*"

"You ask them," said Matt, "That is the obvious answer."

"While you cannot be so direct and crass to ask, *'what do you want, why do you want it and when will you buy'*, you are correct that questions are the key to determining them. Some selling experts say engage the client in a pure questioning model, some say Socratic selling, and others subscribe to behavioral models like SPIN® selling as the most effective. Each in their own right has a place, but I have found a simple, more natural model to help people open up. It is simply… *Relax, Relate, and Release.*"

Matt believed that LeRoy had an acronym or alliteration for every situation. He continued to listen and take notes intently. LeRoy continued, "I believe that clients have a sixth sense, much like a cat, a child, or a senior, *like me.* They know your intent, whether it be the commission or your mission. *Would you agree that Mr. Jacobs sensed your anxiety at your meeting?*"

"Yes, stupid rookie was probably written all over my face," Matt answered sheepishly.

"*What was your anxiety based on?*" LeRoy asked already knowing the answer.

"It was the fear of not making the sale, or worse, making a mistake," Matt offered.

"Mr. Jacobs picked up on that vibe and that created an environment that was not conducive to building a relationship or selling a needed/desired product. You have to *relax* and take all the pressure off of the process. You have to detach from the outcome and never be in a big hurry to solve problems or meet needs…that time will present itself."

"*How do I take my mind off everything and relax?*"

"If you were wealthy and commission was not important, *then why would you be there?*"

"I would be there strictly to serve. I get it…I have to detach from the personal gain of the transaction and focus on the needs and desires of the client."

"Exactly! Number two is *relating*. We said a couple of days ago, that the most important thing to a client is solving a problem or meeting a desire. To relate means to build rapport, to genuinely empathize with their position. You begin slowly engaging them in open ended conversation that gets them to say more than just 'yes' or 'no'. Relating is conversational and provides clues and cues for you to follow in a systematic but natural progression."

"It sounds hard," Matt interjected, "How do I remain relaxed and relate when deep down I am trying to sell something that I believe is good for them?"

"Remember your round of golf with your friends and whiffing the tee shot?"

"*How could I forget?* I felt the same way with Mr. Jacobs the other day. I totally whiffed that meeting!" Matt said now laughing at his performance.

"How does it feel over your tee shot today - natural, I presume?" LeRoy was once again leading the witness down the primrose path.

"With golf I am confident in what I know and my experience."

"You will have to apply the same approach here. At times, it will feel unnatural but with time and practice you will build the same confidence in these two stages of the professional sales process," LeRoy explained.

Matt knew he was right. He is no longer anxious at the first tee shot. He recalled once in a tournament when he was playing with a well known PGA professional. He was not nervous at all. In fact, he was more anxious to show his stuff.

LeRoy pulled him out of his daydreaming with the words, "Finally, there is *release*. Once you have set the atmosphere of relaxation, and related to the point of your understanding *what* they need and *why* they need it, then, and only then, can you release your solution. When done properly, the *when will they buy* becomes now. The relevant objections have been handled in the first two phases and as long as your product meets the discovered and uncovered needs, you would have secured a client."

Matt was starting to get a full picture of the sales process and realized that while he had not demonstrated any level of basic proficiency, he had all the raw materials to make a go of it. As he reflected on his interaction with Mr. Jacobs, he could see each place he took a wrong turn. *He couldn't wait until he had another opportunity with a new client.*

Friday - Lunch #15 What do you know the client doesn't?

For Matt, it had been an exhausting week, and he was truly glad it was Friday. Two days to catch his breath without the overseeing eye of his sales manager and director. While they were nice enough, and were only trying to be supportive of the teams, all the "rah-rah" was tiring - *especially since he wasn't very productive*. Ok, maybe he was feeling just a little bit sorry for himself based on the horrendous meeting with Mr. Jacob.

"Happy Friday!" shouted LeRoy as he walked down the sidewalk to the cafe. Matt knew that their reasons of gratitude for it being the end of the week, were quite different, but he agreed...Friday...*at last!*

"I see a man that has had a rough week. Let's go easy today, alright?" LeRoy said compassionately.

If he had really wanted to go easy on Matt, maybe he wouldn't take the crisp $10 out of his pocket today. Fat chance of that as LeRoy was already enjoying warm bread with butter and the birds were already dancing just a few feet away. With this idyllic scene, all Matt could offer was, "Yes, please go easy on me today."

"*Tell me, what do you know that the client doesn't?*" LeRoy asked jumping into the lesson before Matt's lack of energy could take root.

"Well, after my experience this week, I don't think there is *anything* they don't know...*seems like the client holds all the cards*."

"As we have discussed, the needs and desires of the client are surely paramount, but there is something *we know* that they don't. Again I ask, what is that?" It was evident that LeRoy was not going to join in on Matt's Friday afternoon pity party.

"I don't know, *our products* I guess," he said half interested.

"That is correct. <u>That is where you should be the expert</u>. Once you are ready to Release your solutions, it is time for you to demonstrate your prowess regarding your products. There are two key things you must understand about your product and how they integrate into your mission of helping people build generational wealth. *They are features and benefits*."

"What about the competition or price?" he asked working to gain interest.

"The two factors I just outlined will be *the key* to gaining an edge against competitors. I never bring up or talk about competition with my clients."

"What if they ask about them or how our product compares?"

"Make no mistake, as the professional seller, you must understand your competitor, making note of their superiority and vulnerabilities. But I will not engage in what I like to call the *burger wars* and take away from my objectivity regarding *my products*," LeRoy countered.

"*Burger wars?*" now Matt was having his interest sparked.

"I do not like commercials where Burger King® and McDonalds® show their burgers side-by-side, one disparaging the other. In some ways, you insult people when you limit their choices. Tell me, which do you prefer - a flame broiled Whopper® or two all beef patties, special sauce, lettuce, cheese -"

"Pickles onions on a sesame seed bun - the Big Mac®!" Matt finished. Now he was smiling and laughing at the real life relevance of how a product is marketed and positioned in the mind of a potential client. He answered, "There are times when I like *both* of them."

"Exactly! *So why would I complicate your options by bringing up my competitor in a negative way?* If the client truly wants to compare, I will demonstrate *my solutions fully* but then recommend they contact the competitor directly for them to give a full demonstration as well."

"You take the high road, right?"

"That is correct. I refuse to get engaged in a head-to-head war. *I have to live with losing a sale when another company's solution was deemed better in the mind of the client than mine.* I would not maintain that business long anyway if I won by sheer force of will or skill if my product doesn't meet their needs. Even I will never close 100% of the time, so my primary goal is to explain to my client the features and benefits of *my products.*"

"I have been reading about benefits and features for weeks now," Matt conveyed.

"Then *you* tell me what they are and the differences," he instructed.

For the first time in 3 weeks, LeRoy was allowing him to run the discussion. Matt seized the opportunity and began, "*Features describe the characteristics of our product and benefits describe how the features meet the client's specific needs or desires.*"

"Whoa, somebody has been reading the sales training manual! I am impressed! *Which one is most important to the client?*"

"Benefits of course, as they detail how the product will solve their specific problem, their needs and desires," Matt said proudly.

"Masterfully explained - you should spend the majority of your Release segment, describing benefits and how they will help the client. *No one wants to hear a bullet by bullet description of every feature.* At the moment of purchase, the benefits demonstrated for specifically discovered and uncovered needs should be your *main focus.*"

"*What about price?*" Matt asked.

"What about it?" LeRoy asked, probing Matt to think deeper.

"Doesn't price matter?"

"Of course it matters, but it is not the greatest factor, particularly in a complex sale. *If price was the single greatest factor, the* _cheapest products_ *would always win, right?*"

"Yes, that makes sense. While we don't always have the *lowest price*, that doesn't stop Larry Wilcox and others from securing clients daily," said Matt getting revelation.

"Another real example for you - do you drink Gatorade®?"

"Yes, there is nothing better when you are playing golf in the hot sun," Matt answered.

"Let's talk about the price. How much does a bottle of Gatorade cost?" asked LeRoy.

"That depends on *where you buy it*. My buddies and I are perplexed by how much the price changes with the environment."

"Expound on that please...*different prices in different environments?*"

"Well, if we stop on the way *to* the golf course, the grocery store sells them for $1.00 for a 32oz bottle. That is typically the best price. If we get it at the local gas station, it is a $1.69 for the same 32oz bottle. If we buy that same bottle at the Fulbright campus golf course, it is $2.00 - twice the price of the grocery store."

"Very interesting. *What happens to the price if you play at the country club where you want to live?*" LeRoy asked.

"Oh, then it gets crazy at $3.00 for a 20oz bottle...*plus* you have to tip the cart person!" Matt shouted calling out the obvious inequity of the pricing structure.

"Then I suppose you show your displeasure by *not* drinking Gatorade in those higher priced environments, right?" queried LeRoy already knowing the answer.

Matt shook his head ,started laughing and answered, "*No, call us crazy, but we still buy it.*"

"I will tell you why...*the answer is value.* Price divided by benefits equal value. *Value is what everyone is looking for in any transaction.* A child might buy 3 for a $1.00 chocobars and pass up the $.75 cost for *one* Snickers® bar. In that transaction, *quantity is the key driver...not quality.* What might that same child do if Snickers were on sale; 2 for $1.00 or better yet, the same 3 for $1.00 as the chocobars?"

"The kid will likely buy Snickers in the last two scenarios, *right?*" Matt asked knowing his own personal answer.

"Very likely, because the *potent combination of price, benefits, and enjoyment come together to create an experience.* <u>That is the real key - *Do not allow your product to become a commodity.*</u> The price may be fixed, and benefits may be defined, *but enjoyment of the process is the variable that you can control.* It becomes the differentiator that sets you apart from lower priced competition who is depending on price as their main advantage. *Turn your solutions into a wonderful experience and you will win consistently.*"

Monday - Lunch #16 Become a cultivator

While others took their morning break, Matt stayed hard at work on the phone. While he had some strong possibilities, nothing had firmed up yet. The sales manager and the director both noticed his effort and tried to re-assure him that it was a matter of time, and to just keep working at it. He recalled LeRoy's Law of Averages lesson and knew they were right - it would happen, *had* to happen for him soon. He was no longer envious when the other newbie's rang the bell for securing appointments. *He knew his time would come and their success meant his was possible, too.*

It was noontime and he was heading to the cafe to meet LeRoy. He was welcomed by the cafe owner and before he knew it he said, "Happy Monday!"

"Well, I'll be," said the owner, "LeRoy is truly rubbing off on you!"

Matt realized that he had said it almost unconsciously and replied, "Let's not tell LeRoy about this."

"It will be our little secret, but you could do worse than emulate Mr. LeRoy."

LeRoy was already sitting down enjoying a glorious day when he said to Matt, trying to catch him off guard, "There is more to the sales process than closing the sale. *What do you think that is?*"

"Staying in contact with your client," he answered quickly.

"Correct! What happens <u>after the sale</u> is infinitely more important that all that happened before. Similar to our simplified sales process of Relax, Relate, Release, we have 3 more R's to cover. They are *Reinforce, Referrals, and Repeat*."

Matt wondered how many more words could possibly start with "R" and then laughed to himself and wrote the words down quickly.

"Let me ask you, have you ever bought anything that didn't work the way you expected or you had trouble understanding all the features?" LeRoy asked.

"Yes, just recently that happened."

"What did you do?"

"I called the company that made the product to get help from their customer service department."

"How did that go?"

"Not so good," Matt recalled. "I was on hold for 10 minutes, they asked me a lot of useless questions and at the end of everything they emailed me a list of troubleshooting hints and said call back if those things don't work."

"Did they work?"

"Of course not, and I pride myself on being tech savvy," Matt answered in an agitated tone.

"So, what did you do then?"

"I took the unit back to the store for a refund," he said firmly.

"Precisely what happens in most cases when the client buys but isn't satisfied. Now let me tell you about my experience buying a laptop. *You didn't think I owned one, did you?*" LeRoy asked in a self-deprecating voice.

"Well, they do call you *the old dinosaur* in the office," Matt said feigning disgust at his office mates. He had been holding onto that nickname for three weeks.

"T-Rex I hope! No matter. Anyway, I bought the computer from a very nice young sales professional named Tyrone, much like yourself, who took the time to ask exactly what I would be doing with the laptop. I told him I would do occasional emails and videos. He recommended something called Skype® so that I could not only talk to, but see, my daughter RoseMarie in Aruba. I told him I would also do a little light surfing on the web and that was all. He recommended a mid-priced unit that he said would provide both power and simplicity based on my needs. He spent over an hour with me and was fabulous. I thanked him for his patience and professionalism and then checked out."

He continued to relay his experience, "When I got home, all was as he said - simple and easy to set up - *except the video*. I remembered what he said to me as I went to the cashier, 'If you have any problems, call me *first* and I will either assist you myself or get someone who can. We want you to be satisfied with your purchase.' I called Tyrone and he walked me through a few simple things and within 15 minutes, I was talking to him face to face on the computer! I was so excited, amazed and grateful for his support."

It was obvious LeRoy was not yet finished, excited to relay a positive story, "I called the store manager to give Tyrone a raving fan review. I said to the store manager that the young man was earning his commission and that he was a great asset to their company. *What do you think the manager said to me?* It will blow your mind!"

Matt knew that he wanted him to guess, "He said that Tyrone was the top sales person? He was being promoted to manager? Had he won an all expenses paid trip to Disney World® ...*what?*"

"He said that their associates *don't* earn commission. *They pay them based on complete customer satisfaction.* They make more money, *not* if the customer buys, but only if the customer is 100% satisfied. *Is that mad or what?*"

"When I think about it, *it's brilliant.* Service has become a dying art in many businesses. That doesn't really apply to us, because we only get paid on selling products so service is not as important," Matt conveying his opinion on the impact to his business.

"Not exactly. *What if your client returns the product?* What if they don't tell their friends how great you and your products are, *or worse*, they tell them how bad your product and your service were? What if they never do business with you again? *What do you lose?*" inquired LeRoy in rapid succession to help him see the bigger picture.

"I lose a client, my commission, renewals, and future opportunities with them," Matt now realizing that *anything* that goes wrong would impact him greatly. <u>Even those things he couldn't control</u>.

"But most importantly, Matt, you lose your reputation. So let's review the last 3 R's shall we? Reinforce - the most positive time in a prospect's mind is after they make a purchase...*it is also the most vulnerable.*"

"*Why?* They should be happy after a good purchase," offered Matt.

"Certainly, they will be happy, but they will naturally second guess the decision of their purchase. They will tell a trusted friend what they have done for feedback and the secret need for approval. They will check the internet to see what strangers have done, how they have rated the product and strangers experiences to compare it to their own."

"You know, you are right," said Matt. "I bought new golf clubs a year ago and I kept checking the internet to see what people said about them or if I could get them at a cheaper price, *even though everything went perfectly.* I can only imagine what might happen if things don't go just right."

"What is the best thing a professional seller can do in this vulnerable period? <u>Reinforce the good decision the client has just</u>

<u>made</u>. You do this by sending them a thank you card. Calling them once the product is received to make sure all is well and if they have any questions. I have a tickler file that alerts me to check in with clients on critical dates of delivery, special future dates in their lives, and anniversary dates. I don't overwhelm them but simply let them know, I have not, and will not abandon them *after the sale.*"

"You reinforce," affirmed Matt.

"Exactly!"

Matt, anticipating what was next asked, "When do you ask for the next 'R' - *referrals?*"

"I know that classic, traditional sales training dictates that you ask for them immediately once the sale is consummated. Certainly, under the right conditions clients would be in such a state of euphoria that they will provide them. *I personally prefer to obtain them once I have demonstrated a high level of professional excellence and the client is happy with the product.* Believe me, if you satisfy the client and reinforce the sale through service, they will open doors to their family, friends, colleagues and co-workers in a way that business meets you at your desk every day. *Then you transition from a producer to a cultivator.*

"It will also be important to thank them, personally if possible, for *every* opportunity they send you," LeRoy continued. "Even if that referral doesn't become a client, showing appreciation and gratitude are vital. Just as you thank Erin for a clean home, a great home cooked meal; it shows you value her and what she does. Gratitude and appreciation also shows the universe that you are happy with full loaves of bread, and -"

"*Crumbs from the Master's Table*," Matt intuitively finishing his thought remembering LeRoy's impassioned statement from the first day.

"The final 'R' is *Repeat*. If you remain in contact with the client over time, along with the referrals you will receive, you will get the call that their needs have changed. Or in your annual reviews of their situation, you determine there is a better solution for the changing times. While some people will be set for a lifetime with your solutions, others will have life changing events...births, deaths, marriages, etc. *Who do you want them to think of at these critical stages in their lives?*"

"Me!" Matt said elatedly.

"Absolutely! As a sales professional, you want to position yourself in the minds of your clients as their *trusted advisor*. They may not need you for years, but when they do, *you* should be there. When another company tries to come in and replace the solutions you have developed -"

"*I want them to call me!*" Matt said defending his honor and hard work.

"By Jove, I think he's got it! Be clear, this is not a rat race where we fight or compete over clients. *True sales success lies in developing natural chemistry, providing solutions, and servicing that solution for a lifetime.* It is a commitment, but as we have seen, the rewards are great!"

"*Emancipation, Gratification and Remuneration*!" exclaimed the proud student.

"Ok...ok...now you are just showing off. I believe you are almost ready!"

Tuesday - Lunch #17 If at first you don't succeed!

L eRoy jumped into the daily session realizing that time was drawing nigh on their lessons. "*If I could only give you one word that would demonstrate the personal quality that provided me with the greatest results over the years, that word would be persistence.* Not the kind of persistence that makes me a pest or nuisance, mind you. The kind of persistence that makes me continue to push when the odds and circumstances look against me. The kind of persistence that makes me work on myself when I am tired and the results are not immediate. The kind of persistence that compels me to become an expert in my field, learning how my solutions - my products - can help me accomplish my mission of helping people Eradicate Poverty. *Finally, the kind of persistence that allows me to get up again when I have been knocked down.*" LeRoy had turned up the emphatic meter 5 notches, but Matt understood how important this lesson would be.

"Funny, that sounds like something my father or grandfather would say," Matt realizing that LeRoy and his patriarchs were a lot alike. There is an old school wisdom that puts people first in everything they said and did.

"I am certain they are great men as they have raised a great young man. Right now, right here, today, *what can you do to prove to yourself that you are willing to be persistent and do the uncomfortable things?*"

"Well, it has bothered me all week - I want to call Mr. Jacobs back," he divulged.

"What stops you?" LeRoy asked.

"I don't want to be a pest or a nuisance, as you just said, and Mr. Jacobs had the final word."

"What did he really say 'no' to - *your products or your approach?*"

"Reviewing the last few days of lessons and my notes, it is obvious - *my approach*," Matt acknowledged.

"Do you think he still *needs* and would benefit from what your mission is and the possible solutions you have to offer?"

"Yes, I truly do," said Matt confidently.

"Then you have the conviction necessary to try again. The only question is, *will you?*"

"What would I say?" asked Matt probing for the right words.

"Speak from the heart with honesty and integrity and focus only on servicing and meeting his needs. *Can you do that?*" LeRoy asked.

"Yes, I most certainly can!" Matt now had a new feeling of empowerment and knew that the worst thing that could happen was a little more rejection. *A small price to pay!*

"Then take out your cell phone and call him immediately!" he commanded. "*Never let time get between you and a moment of conviction.* Time and procrastination will only water it down! I will enjoy lunch...go place the call."

Matt excuses himself and goes to make the hardest call he has ever made. "Mr. Jacobs, this is Matt Palmer, I came out to your house last week..."

"Yes, I remember. I am just a little old but not senile!" snapped Mr. Jacobs.

"I won't take much of your time. *The first thing I wanted to do was apologize.* I have to come clean; you are the first client I have ever had. I am fresh out of college and was a little too eager to offer my help. But I don't want my lack of experience to keep you from taking care of something important to you and your family's future."

"I could tell you were still wet behind the ears. Tell me, where did you go to school?" he asked trying to see if he was telling the truth.

"I got my degree from Fulbright College upstate."

"I have a grandson that is looking to go there in the Fall. *Is it a good school?*"

Absolutely! It was the best 4 years of my life. I got my degree, met my wife, and made so many good friends. What is your grandson's name?"

"His name is Thomas Jacobs and he is one of my oldest son's children," he responded.

"Mr. Jacobs, tell Thomas he can call me if he wants to get the inside scoop on Fulbright," Matt offered sincerely.

"Now you are just being nice cause you want me to buy life insurance. I don't like being manipulated!" Mr. Jacobs was still on high guard.

"No sir, I would talk to Thomas regardless. I am always happy to get another alumnus for Fulbright. *I believe in the school and want to continue to support it.* They have a great curriculum, a great athletic program on a wonderful campus and in a safe environment."

"I have to tell you Matt, you sound different talking about Fulbright" said Mr. Jacobs, his natural defenses beginning to come down slightly.

"I guess because it is something I am passionate about and know it would be good for your grandson and anyone that attended. The same way I know if you allow me, I can do a better job explaining how I can help you build generational wealth for Thomas and other members of your family...*if you will allow me another visit.*"

"*Generational wealth?*" asked Mr. Jacobs now intrigued with Matt's mission statement.

"Yes sir," instinctively knowing it was time for him to listen.

"One of my goals is to take care of my children and their children, *but I don't want to be sold anything I don't need!*" That was followed by a silence that felt like years. Mr. Jacobs then breaks the cold silence, "Okay Matt, come see me tomorrow...at 10am sharp!"

"Yes, sir, I will be there at 10am and thank you for the opportunity to serve you!"

Matt was ecstatic. He quickly went to LeRoy to share the news, when almost clairvoyantly LeRoy asked, "*What time do you meet him?*"

"How did you know?"

"Once a man is convicted and *acts* on that conviction, he will be successful in whatever he puts his hands to do," LeRoy said vehemently.

"*Can you go with me this time?*"

"No Matt. Tomorrow you go by yourself, *but you will not be alone.* The spirit of these lessons will be with you. Trust me, you are ready."

"He wants to meet at 10am sharp, so I will not be at lunch tomorrow," Matt said half-heartedly looking for a reprieve that he knew was not likely to come.

LeRoy said right on cue, "That is a shame. Please leave a $20 bill for today and tomorrow."

Matt could only laugh at the logic...and he gladly paid.

Wednesday - Lunch #18 The student at work

Matt was determined not to be late for this meeting so he hung out at a coffee shop that was right around the corner arriving there at 9am. He bought a coffee and muffin as he remembered that LeRoy always told him to support business, both large and small. He used the time to think of helping Mr. Jacobs and relaxing himself as LeRoy had instructed. He had jotted down some notes about Fulbright College and had a brochure with the phone number to his guidance counselor that he would share with Thomas, Mr. Jacob's grandson. For now, that was all he had, but surprisingly, was all he *felt he needed*. He knocked on the door precisely at 10am.

"Good thing you are on time, I was going to wait 5 minutes then leave to do my shopping," stated Mr. Jacobs.

"Thank you for seeing me, I truly appreciate it."

"I am still not sure why I called you back out here, cause I don't need no more life insurance."

Matt resisted the immediate inclination to offer a sales pitch about the importance of family protection, asset preservation and the inevitability of death. Instead he offered, "Here is a brochure for Thomas and the phone number to my guidance counselor who helped me graduate on time." Matt noticed a picture on the mantle, "*Is this him?*"

"No, that is another grandson, Kyle," said Mr. Jacobs proudly, "He is just a high school junior."

"Wow, he looks college ready! I see the letterman's jacket, what's his sport?"

"He fancies all of them, but his main two are baseball and golf," as he picked up a couple more photos of Kyle in action, showing them to Matt.

"*Golf?* Now you really have my attention. Do you know his handicap?" he asked truly interested.

"I'm not much into the golf talk but he made it to state finals two years in a row, so I know he must be good. *Sounds like you are a golfer?*"

"Yes, sir. I got bitten by the bug in college. Fulbright has a good golf program and a local course where they let the students play for $5 a round. To this day I am still hooked, and since I am an alumnus, I can still play for $5."

"Bet your wife doesn't like you out all day hanging with the boys, huh?" sneered Mr. Jacobs.

"Actually, I take her with me. She rides in the cart and we talk and enjoy the beauty and serenity of the course."

"Good man, never leave your wife alone too long. How long have you been married?" he asked.

"Just over two years and we are expecting our first child in a couple of months."

"Congratulations young man, how does it feel?" he asked with a sincere sense of interest.

"I am nervous and excited at the same time. Getting married was a big step but a child is almost overwhelming," Matt realizing that now Mr. Jacobs seemed to be asking all the questions and was directing the meeting. It felt natural so he wasn't concerned at all about the conversation. *They certainly didn't get this far last time.*

"Don't you worry, you will do fine," Mr. Jacobs said in a reassuring tone.

"How many children do you have?" asked Matt.

"Elma and I have 4 children and 8 grandchildren and counting..."

"Wow, do most of them live in the area?"

"Yes, most of them have remained close to home. Just close enough to see them often, but far enough they have to call first before they come!" He burst out into laughter and Matt laughed genuinely along with him. *Mr. Jacobs seemed different from the other day.* This all felt natural, and then he remembered LeRoy's lesson. Mr. Jacobs was the same, *he* was different - relaxed and relating...creating natural chemistry.

"Now I know Thomas is college age and Kyle is close...what about the other grandchildren?" Matt asked.

"Thomas at 18 and the others range in ages from 4 to 15. We are blessed as they are all good kids," he relayed with his sense of family on full display.

"Tell me Mr. Jacobs, if you could do something special for them, *what would it be?*" trying to work in his reason for coming out again.

"I told you I didn't want to buy no insurance! I am too young to think about dying and don't need you selling me a monthly premium reminder about dying!" said an obviously frustrated Mr. Jacobs.

Now he was the Mr. Jacobs that Matt remembered from the other day. This time he realized his objection was not life insurance, *it was the thought of dying.* He said with all the sincerity of his mission, "Mr. Jacobs, I know you are a proud and honorable man. I can see by the interest you take in your family, the hard work and devotion and all that you sacrificed, that you want the best for them - today and 50 years from now...*right?*" A groan is all he heard back from Mr. Jacobs.

"*Can I share a personal story?* My father is a great man and he provided all he could for my family but when it was time for me to go to Fulbright, my parents could not afford to send me. Right as I graduated high school, my grandfather, we call him Grandbooty -"

Mr. Jacobs interrupted him, "Forgive me...*you call him Grandbooty?*"

"Let me explain, he has a deep cleft in his chin and as children we said that it looked like he had a little butt on his chin. *So we called him Grandbooty!* Been doing it ever since." He laughed at how strange that must have sounded, but it must have been okay, because now Mr. Jacobs was laughing heartily, too.

"Go on with your story...*Grandbooty?*"

"Yes, he came to my high school graduation and handed my dad 10 stock certificates. They were Microsoft® stock he purchased when I was just one years old. He paid $210 for them in 1986 and he left them at the broker all those years. *When he handed them to my dad, they were worth close to $100,000!* They paid my way and my sister's way through college and bought me the car that I drive to this very day."

"I would have paid anything to see the look on his face!" he said slapping his knee with excitement.

"*His face?* It was the first time I had seen *my* father cry in over a decade. My sister and I were dancing and jumping all over the place. *It took all the pressure of money off of our getting an education,*" he says recalling that day fondly.

"So then you are here, *with me today*, because of your grandfa...I mean Grandbooty?"

Matt realized that his story was not just a sales pitch but had represented a materialization of his own personal mission - his grandfather had passed on Generational Wealth. He stood motionless for a moment and said proudly, "*Yes, I am here because of him.*"

"Matt, those are the type of things I want to do for my family. *I want to leave a legacy.* I want to leave -"

"Generational wealth," added Matt finishing his sentence gently.

"Yes, exactly and I like those words, *generational wealth - but* where do I find a Microsoft in all of today's mess? I am not ashamed to say I am a little more than scared of what's happening with banks and all the financial turmoil. *How can I do it?*" There was vulnerability in his voice that Matt realized needed assurances.

"That is what we will figure out, *together*. If you will allow me to be a part in creating that future, we will take a step by step approach to creating that legacy. Just like my Grandbooty, what you do today will provide a huge impact on the future of those you love. We will create a plan that's based on you being there to see that priceless look on their faces, but we will also plan -"

"For just in case of my..." said Mr. Jacobs trying to finish Matt's thought.

He couldn't finish the statement, but Matt realized that wasn't important anymore, so he says in a confirming voice, "Yes, just in case."

"Matt, I am ready, and I believe you are the man to help me do it!"

"Then, let's get started!" Matt said jubilantly.

For the next hour, Matt gathered vital information about Mr. Jacobs. He would take it back to his office, run it through the financial analysis programs and come back with a solution to make Mr. Jacobs' desires a reality. They talked along the way about family, their wives, and Mr. Jacobs dispensed advice about raising children. At the end of their time together, Matt thanked Mr. Jacobs, who shook his hand and held on to it at the door.

"Matt, I have to tell you, I am a little nervous. I am normally scared of making big money moves. I want to do the right thing...*I am trusting you.*"

"Mr. Jacobs, I will also admit, I am a little scared and understand the great responsibility you have given me. *I will never make promises that I can't keep.* I will work until I find the solutions that best suit your individual situation and we will agree on them every step of the way...*agreed?*"

"Yes, agreed," said Mr. Jacobs assured in the process that Matt had outlined.

Matt got into his car. It was as if he had changed in the last 3 hours. It was a metamorphosis brought on by the culmination of all LeRoy had instilled and the knowledge that he had gained through experience. Sure, it was just one transaction and there was still work to be done, but he felt good, he felt confident, but more importantly, *he felt grateful!*

Thursday - Lunch #19 The first sale!

That night, Matt poured over all the information that Mr. Jacobs had provided and began scouring the products that were best suited for him. It was amazing that features he memorized to pass company tests were now coming to life as he thought of how they would help Mr. Jacobs' family. He thought of that pivotal decision when Grandbooty purchased the Microsoft stock that had changed his and his sister's life. The magnitude of it all kept him up late into the night until he felt he had the perfect solution.

That morning, he went into the sales manager to show him the proposal for Mr. Jacobs. The sales manager was impressed and gave it his approval - a requirement for all rookie sales people. Matt had set an 11am appointment with Mr. Jacobs to go over the plan, so he knew he would not make lunch with LeRoy. He went by the cafe early and left a note with the owner to give LeRoy and he was off to see Mr. Jacobs.

When he arrived Mr. Jacobs was openly excited and said, "I didn't sleep much last night thinking about all the things we discussed and the legacy I am about to build."

"I have to admit, I didn't sleep much either but I think I have put together a plan that will do all that you desire, and then some. You have done some really good things already and while it may have been conservative, you put money away consistently. You are to be congratulated for your discipline."

"Yes sir, my father taught me that every dollar you earn is a chance to do good, live good, and save good so you can do more of *all* of those when you get old. I have had some rough patches but I stuck to it regardless of my circumstances."

"Well that makes our work a lot easier. Let me show you what I came up with."

Matt enthusiastically explained his plan line by line to Mr. Jacobs, who asked a lot of questions. Matt evoked the patience of Tyrone, the computer salesman that LeRoy spoke so highly of. No matter how small the detail, he truly wanted Mr. Jacobs to be satisfied.

On the other side of town, LeRoy went to the cafe and at 12:05 was a little vexed that Matt had not shown up yet. He whispered under his breath, "One of the first signs of excellence is keeping your commitments." He was just about to call Matt on his cell phone when the cafe owner came over with an envelope addressed to LeRoy. Inside was a note that said "Gone Cultivating...enjoy lunch!" Inside was a crisp $10 bill! LeRoy laughed out loud and was relieved that all he tried to instill and what he perceived about Matt was valid and true. He enjoyed lunch as he always had. He was thinking positive thoughts about his student and his friend. He was a little nostalgic remembering those same moments of "firsts" in his own life.

After 3 hours, Matt and Mr. Jacobs had finished going over everything. Each stage of Matt's plan had been reviewed, discussed and debated. Finally Mr. Jacobs scratched his head and said, "Matt, this sounds like a mighty fine plan and you have done your best to explain it to me. I understand everything, but I have to admit, I am still a little anxious."

Then Matt said intuitively, "You remind me of my dad. He says there are two ways to make a *good decision* - trust your gut or sleep on it. I know we have covered a lot and it could be overwhelming. I need you to feel confident *before* you do anything. Maybe you should sleep on it."

Mr. Jacob's jumped up from the table like he was shot out of a cannon, "Son, you just said the same thing *my father* said to me...trust your instincts or your pillow! I am trusting my instincts and I am ready, so let's make this happen."

Matt dutifully filled out all the paperwork, dotted every "I" and crossed every "T". At 4pm, they shook hands and Mr. Jacobs put his hand on Matt's shoulder and said, "Matt, for the first time in a long time, I feel like my future and the future of my loved ones are in good hands. For that, I truly thank you."

"No, Mr. Jacobs, I appreciate the trust and confidence you have shown me and giving me the privilege to be a part of creating generational wealth and a legacy for your family. *I am truly honored.*"

Had this been a movie, they would have burst into tears and hugged each other. Each man relieved that something that had felt so far out of reach, *was now in their grasp.* As he got in his car, Matt carefully put away all the documents and immediately called his wife Erin to share the news. She reaffirmed her belief and support of "her hero" and told him dinner would be ready when he got home - and *something special.* The sense of pride and accomplishment was greater than he could bear. As a sense of fulfillment overcame him, he did something he hadn't done in a long time - *he cried tears of joy!*

Friday - Lunch #20 The last lesson

Today was the 20th lunch and Matt realized he had been given more than he could ever have expected in his sessions with LeRoy. *He could hardly wait to tell him about the sale.* Just as he was walking up to the table where LeRoy had already been the last 15 minutes, LeRoy's face lit up and he said excitedly, "Ahhh, the professional seller has arrived! Tell me something good!"

Matt, pretended to be somber to build suspense.

"You can't fool me," LeRoy exclaimed, "I can smell a sale a mile away! Congratulations and welcome to the club of professional sellers!"

"How did you know?"

"It is written all over your face. It is in how you walk, how you carry yourself. It is the gait of a confident man...a successful man."

"You would be correct on all counts. *Today, I turned in my first sale!*" Matt was almost bursting from pride and excitement.

"Wonderful! Now you will begin selling like mad. Nothing creates success like success."

"You know LeRoy, *I feel successful.* It is not even important the size of the account or my commission, but it is the relationship bond that I know I have formed with Mr. Jacobs that is the most satisfying."

"Excellent! Remember now, reinforce, obtain referrals and repeat business," LeRoy reminding him of a recent lesson. He too, was proud knowing he played a part in this pivotal moment in the young man's life.

"Funny thing, I told Mr. Jacobs that once he was satisfied and all was in order, that if he knew others I could help, I would deem it an honor if he could introduce us."

"Good man, cultivate like your life depends on it. Eventually, he will -"

Matt cut LeRoy off unexpectedly, "Well, he already talked to his 4 children about me because he was so excited to tell them how he had planned for their future!"

"*What*? Outstanding!" interjected LeRoy.

"Then he wants me to speak to his Rotary Club to introduce me to several people who need what I have done for him."

"Ok, now who is the master and who is the student? I am very proud of you," LeRoy said sincerely.

Those words resonated in Matt's mind in a way that created a stronger bond between him and LeRoy. Part teacher/student, part father/son, and now, colleague to colleague. He then said to LeRoy, "It would not have been possible without you. I can't express what these last 30 days have meant and the impact to my life. *I am not sure how to repay you.*"

"You do not have to repay, because you have already paid - *lunch x 20*. The only other thing I require is that you succeed wildly. Always doing the right things, for the right reasons, at all times. I know that great success is your destiny. *It is also fitting that today is our last formal lesson as I will not see you for a while.*"

"*What do you mean? Where are you going?*" Matt asked truly concerned.

"No worries, I have to travel back to Guyana and take care of some long overdue business. For some reason, I have been putting it off for years, but now feel released to go. Rest assured, you will see me again - you won't get rid of an old man that easily. Also be confident in the fact that you have all the qualities of a great sales professional and even more importantly, the character of a great man. *Do you deem me qualified to make that judgment?*" LeRoy asked in earnest.

"Yes, but that doesn't change the fact that I will miss you - I have learned to lean on you through these sessions," Matt responded with his emotions on visible display.

"All the more reason for me to leave for a while. Orison Swett Marden said it best - '*Nothing else so destroys the power to stand alone as the habit of leaning upon others. If you lean, you will never be strong or original. Stand alone or bury your ambition to be somebody in the world.*'"

"I understand and do believe that I am ready for the next level of life and what it will teach me. You still owe me one more impartation to clear your ledger...*what is the lesson today?*" Matt thinking some great wisdom would be imparted on this final day.

"Lesson? You get no lesson today. You are now a bona fide sales professional. *We are now colleagues.* May I buy *you* lunch?"

"Yes, that would be great. I heard the food here is good, *but I have never eaten here before,*" Matt said jokingly.

The cafe owner said to them, "Can I interest you in bread?" And in unison, LeRoy and Matt said, "Yes, you can always interest me in bread...warm with butter, please."

It was a bitter sweet moment for Matt as he enjoyed lunch with his good friend, not knowing when he would see him again. He also knew that *he* wasn't the same person he was just 30 days ago. He felt the change that had enveloped his mind coursing through his entire body and knew it would only be a matter of time before it would begin permeating his outer circumstances. As LeRoy had just told him, it was time to spread his wings and begin the journey to the next level of success. As LeRoy proceeded to feed the birds and they danced with delight, Matt realized that the strength of his new <u>vision</u> would always bring him <u>provision</u>...*even if it is just Crumbs from the Master's Table.*

Epilogue - A final crumb

The next several weeks were chaotic and eventful...all leading to the crescendo of the birth of his daughter, closing the biggest sales of his career, and delivering the top new sales person address to a class of newbies. The Monday morning sales meeting was about to begin and life was almost back to normal, albeit *very busy* - the new normal for Matt.

LeRoy was also scheduled to be back in the office from his weeks in Guyana and Matt was excited to get to see him to tell him all that had happened while he was gone. The Sales VP was back in the office and Matt wondered what could be happening *this time*. He then noticed that he and LeRoy were shaking hands. The VP stood at the front of the room and addressed the team. He informed them that LeRoy was officially retiring after 30 years of faithful and productive service. There was even a letter from the company president! Matt went to LeRoy after the obligatory well wishes from people who had never taken the time to get to know him.

"Why didn't you tell me?" Matt asked working hard to keep hold of his emotions.

"I didn't know until after our last lunch," began LeRoy also holding *his emotions* at bay. "I will still service my faithful clients, but have decided to relax and enjoy my family more - travel and a life of leisure. Before I could sail into that sunset, I had to have a confirmation and an assurance that there would be at least *one* person here who could carry on my mission and do it with a high degree of integrity and professionalism. *That person is you.* I thank you for allowing me to be a small part of your life. A Crumb..."

Matt finishes the statement, *"From the Master's Table."* Matt couldn't believe it was all happening so fast. "Can we keep up with each other...maybe over lunch?"

"Of course, a man should never work on an empty stomach! Remember all that I have taught you, and remember, no matter what - *your mission!* I have great faith in you and have full assurance that you will accomplish everything you set your hand to do. God Bless!"

They shook hands warmly and shared a manly embrace. With no fanfare or gold watch, LeRoy left as anonymously as he had worked the past three decades. Matt felt a little empty as he watched him leave but knew he was right. He had just been handed the baton and had to live up to the promise.

A sense of urgency and eagerness filled his heart and mind as he moved to occupy his seat at the table with 4 phones - which quickly turned into a cube, and within a year as he garnered "rookie of the year" turned into a small office. Within 3 years, Matt was moved to a private office with Anna as his company provided assistant. By his 5th year, he was the first person to be top producer 12 months in a row, where he appropriately had the words 'top producer' changed to 'top cultivator'. Throughout, he was always willing to lend quick advice to the newbies, never forgetting how he had gotten started, but remained focused on the mission he had established with LeRoy at the cafe, *and the lessons that life had taught him about sales and life mastery.*

He and LeRoy kept in touch as promised. They had lunch every month to begin with, but as with all things, life's demands necessitated the meetings become quarterly, and with the passing of years, a much anticipated annual reunion. *A full decade after Leroy's retirement, Matt was now quite successful.* He and his wife Erin were expecting their third child, they just purchased a magnificent home at the country club and every dream they had dreamed was a reality. Of course, he still had his mission and remained focused on it. There had been the opportunities for promotion, but Matt remained true to his calling, knowing it was his "highest and best" use for this stage of his life.

Matt was preparing for the now annual luncheon with LeRoy and he was especially excited to share news of all the happenings of the past year. As he arrived at the cafe, he immediately noticed their usual location was unoccupied. That's odd; LeRoy was always 15 minutes early *wherever* he was going. Matt took his seat and looked around for the cafe owner. He called a familiar face to the table to inquire, "Is the owner here today?"

"No, he will be back shortly," he answered

"I am also looking for LeRoy, my friend, who has come here for many years sitting right in this very spot."

"Oh yes, *the insurance salesman*," answered the waiter.

He must not have known LeRoy with *that* description chuckled Matt thinking to himself. "Yes, that is him."

Just then the cafe owner walks up and greets Matt with a hearty welcome. "Here sits Matthew Palmer, Generational Wealth Specialist," he said like he was announcing royalty. "Mr. LeRoy wanted me to give you this letter and beg forgiveness."

"*Is he ok?*" Matt asked in a worried voice.

"No need to worry, my friend, he is doing fine. Read the letter and all will be explained."

He looked at the envelope and his name, Matthew Palmer was there and underneath it simply said, *One Last Crumb*. As Matt opened the handwritten letter, he got nervous wondering what it could be. The letter was on beautiful parchment paper and written in LeRoy's own handwriting. It began;

Dearest Matthew,

I will be brief as all the important things were said between us 10 years ago over a magical 30 day period. While you credit me with teaching, it was you that taught me more. You taught me that I have a new mission...one of mentorship for others like you. That is why I am going back home to teach others what I know and raise another generation of professional sellers. Thank you for listening to an old man who was filled with age old wisdom.

One more thing, now that I have officially fully retired to my new calling, I need someone to look after my friends who have entrusted their lives to me over the years. Here is a letter I sent to all of my clients;

My friends,

I thank you for allowing me to play a small part in your lives and the lives of those you love. As I transition into another phase of life, I want to introduce you to my kindred spirit - Matthew "Matt" Palmer. He is worthy of your trust and will assist you as I did with a genuine heart and love of service. Please open your lives to him as you did for me.

Health, happiness, and a lot of money!

Conrod Athelstan LeRoy Shuffler

What did it all mean? The cafe owner came over and saw the perplexed look on Matt's face. "What troubles you?" he asks, "Mr. LeRoy has just left you the keys to the Kingdom!"

"What do you mean?"

"As I understand it, Mr. LeRoy just turned over his book of business, his clients, *to you.* You were indeed fortunate to have LeRoy take such interest in you; he is truly a great man! He came to me 40 years ago with this notion of helping me Eradicate Poverty. His wisdom and persistence are the reason I opened my first cafe and subsequently, guided me to start or purchase over 10 businesses - all that have been very successful. I owe him my life. *That is why I would never allow him to pay for lunch.*"

"Pardon me, you mean LeRoy *never* paid for lunch?" Matt asked pretending to be perturbed.

"Not in over 40 years, even though the meal was free for him and his guest - *and he always left a generous $10 tip!* That is the kind of man he is."

Matt burst out into spontaneous laughter. LeRoy was certainly one of a kind. *Now he realizes he could have eaten too!!!*

The cafe owner continued with more revelation, "It might surprise you to know, that he is very wealthy and is very generous to his family and community. As a man who started with nothing, coming to this country with $200 in his wife Pamela's shoe, he rose to heights of greatness in his chosen profession, creating a financial and spiritual legacy for generations to come." Matt was shocked to hear all of this about LeRoy, in over a decade, he *never* said a word of his achievements.

The cafe owner, realizing he had surprised the young man said, "Enough of my going on, you are here, please have lunch – you are now the benefactor of LeRoy's complimentary lifetime of lunches. *The special perhaps? Can I interest you in bread?*"

"You can always interest me in bread, warm with butter please - *In honor of my good friend.*"

As the bread arrived a small group of birds circled close. As Matt finished the crusty roll, he did as he had seen LeRoy do many times. He carefully scraped all the crumbs into his palm and extended the hand of generosity to the gathering flock. To his surprise, the first bird, the second, third and fourth bird gently came to take the offering. As he contemplated the last 10 years and all that has transpired, he has a deeper understanding of life; *A new revelation that was borne out of his years of struggle, hope and success - an irreplaceable wealth of experiences that forged who he was at this moment.* As tears emerged and streamed down his face, his heart danced in unison with the jubilant birds enjoying *their* divine provision. Witnessing this scene afresh, he recalls the question from LeRoy from the first day they met. He looks up into the pristine blue sky and says without reservation and out loud for all to hear...

"Yes, LeRoy, *I believe it.*"

CONTINUE THE ADVENTURE WITH MATT IN THE NEXT STAGE OF HIS JOURNEY WITH THE COMPLETE SALES CRUMBS TRILOGY!

A Special Preview of The Complete Sales Crumbs Trilogy

Chapter One - A Trail of Crumbs

I t was early Sunday afternoon and Matt was at Grandbooty's 1,000 acre farm. It had been in the family over 100 years, passed down from his great-great grandfather. He took great pride in the farm and lovingly called it the "family gathering place". As a family tradition, they had Sunday dinners there after church once a month. The entire family was there; Grandbooty, whose real name was George, his wife Frankie, Matt's parents, Alfred and Sara, Matt's wife, Erin and his sister, Donna. These gatherings were smaller than the impromptu but more frequent get-togethers with Erin's larger family. Both were always fun and Matt truly enjoyed spending time with both sides of his family.

The ladies were all in the kitchen and the men were getting the table ready. The smells emanating from the kitchen always made Matt salivate.

"George, we have a problem," said Frankie with a feigned sense of alarm.

"Alright Frankie, *where's the fire?*" replied George in a 'yes dear' tone.

"We are out of eggs."

"That don't sound like a problem to me," he said nonchalantly.

"Alright, you tell Matt he won't be getting my warm pound cake with homemade ice cream today! *Matt, is that alright with you?* Oh yes...I was going to bake an extra one for you and Erin to take home with you!"

"Houston, we have a *big* problem!!!" Matt exclaimed.

His wife Erin spoke up rubbing his stomach, "Matt, you put the *pound* in pound cake - 25 of them since we got married to be exact!"

"Is that the pot calling the kettle?" Matt responded comically.

"This is baby weight, *your baby* in fact!" Erin interjected, rubbing her own belly now over 7 months pregnant. "That is my excuse and I am sticking with it...*what's yours?*"

Admittedly, he had picked up 25 pounds since Erin had gotten pregnant. Along with the job loss, and the stress of his new position he indulged in habits that weren't exactly healthy. *That didn't matter right now.* Though he had promised Erin he would lose the weight, all he could think about was Frankie's pound cake with ice cream and peaches from the farm!

"I know my son, and by the look on his face, the 'no desert' option isn't on the table for discussion," said Sara.

"Well, if cakes are going to be on the table, I need 6 eggs - the *whole thing* means nothing without eggs," Frankie said maintaining the air of urgency.

"Why are they so important?" Matt asked. "Can't you make it without them?"

"One pound each of flour, butter, sugar won't hold together if you don't *bind* them with eggs!" she explained. "George, go down to the hen house and bring me 6 fresh eggs."

"Alright, I'm going. But Matt, since you will be the benefactor of the extra cake, you come with me," commanded Grandbooty, realizing that his wife of over 50 years would always have the last word.

"Gladly!" said Matt giddily.

As they walked down the road a few football fields to the hen house, Grandbooty asked Matt how work was going. It was going to be a long walk, so Matt relayed how he had struggled the first 2 weeks but then met LeRoy. He summarized how he was mentored by him for 30 days over lunch and how impactful their time together had been. It had only been a week since LeRoy left and he was still trying to make sense of the job and all that he had learned.

"Wow! You certainly have had an eventful start. I am glad to hear it is going better for you."

"I'm not out the woods yet, but I *feel* like I can do it. I can see all the things I need around me, but don't know how to put it together, yet."

As they reached the hen house, Grandbooty carefully took 6 eggs from the nest and put them in a cloth covered basket. There were scores of little chicks flittering around the area right in front of the hen house. Grandbooty took a hand full of a feed and scattered it about. The chicks danced like it was Christmas day, chirping and leaping up in the air. The scene reminded Matt of the first day at the cafe with LeRoy and the two birds. He relayed the story to Grandbooty who shook his head in appreciative acknowledgement.

"I understand how difficult it is trying to put together the pieces of life's puzzle. <u>For a man to find his way with so much on the line is the real challenge</u>. There's one thing *another* old man can tell you that might help you get through life," he offered.

"Please tell me, I am all ears," said Matt sincerely desiring clarity for where he was in his life. He drew in closer as Grandbooty's wisdom was always simple, but somehow *dead on*.

"It is not the big things that show you the way, but the *little things*. To use a cue from LeRoy's first lesson - <u>*life is about the crumbs*</u>. When I want these little chicks to go a certain way, I will spread a trail of crumbs in the direction I want them to go. To get the prize, <u>they must follow the trail</u>. *Life is like that*. Little voices of instruction call to you gently - guiding your path. Some people call it intuition, inspiration and the pastor at church calls it divine revelation. You have to be on the lookout for those crumbs and have the faith to follow them when they appear. Each crumb will take you a little further on your path, and sustain you on the journey."

"That reminds me of my first sale with a man named Mr. Jacobs. Things were going *really bad*, when, instinctively, I began telling him the story of how you bought the Microsoft® stock when I was one years old. I shared how those 10 certificates helped pay mine and Donnas' way through college. Telling that story helped turn the situation around and Mr. Jacob's disposition changed," Matt recounted.

The memory of that day brought a big smile to Grandbooty's face. "I remember that day like it was yesterday. Your father even cried up a storm. I will never forget that day...*it was one of the greatest of my life!*" he reminisced.

"I have to ask you - how did you have the foresight to know to buy that stock all those years ago?" asked Matt trying to gain insight into how a man comes to make critical decisions in his life.

"That's just it - I didn't have any magical insight," he admitted candidly. "I was scared out of my mind of the stock market because of my dad and my grandfather. All they ever talked about was the Great Crash of 1929 and the Depression. It hit'em real hard. They almost lost this farm because the bank couldn't loan him *any money*, even if only to buy seed, *for 3 years*. They didn't trust banks or Wall Street after that".

"How did you get past your fear?"

"I found something more important to focus on - something so precious that it guided me past my developed ignorance and years of fear. Something that required I get over my limitations and get out of my lazy boy chair."

"What was that?" Matt asked intensely interested.

"It was you?"

"*Me?*"

"The day you were born, I looked into your eyes and held that tiny little hand and I knew I had to do something. *Something that would last well beyond my time here on earth.* My dad gave me this farm, as did his father before him and so on. True, your dad broke the generational line when he went off to make his own life in the car business. I have to admit, that hurt me but I understand a man having to blaze his own path. I have learned to respect him for that - it took a while, though."

While Grandbooty and Alfred got along alright, there was a historical tension between them based on that decision. Matt sensed it ever since he was a little boy but *no one* ever talked about it.

"We put our differences aside because you were here and none of that was important. I only wanted to be in your life and do something important for you. Since I realized that you, too, would eventually blaze your own path, I had to give you another legacy...another type of farm...*an education,*" he said reliving all the emotion of the time.

"How did you even know about Microsoft back then?" Matt said to change the intensity of the highly reflective conversation.

"Well, it was truly one of my life's best little trail of crumbs. It seemed to come out of nowhere, but I heeded the voice when it came."

"Tell me what happened."

"Well, I did my banking business down at 1st Federal and a young man, named Jim Maxwell used to always want me to sit down to talk about investments. He must have thought I was rich and educated, because he always made me feel important. He would talk about the coming wave of technology, computers and all that jazz. He must not have known I only got a 6 grade education because he kept it up - almost every time I walked in."

"Was he a pest?" wondered Matt as he knew persistence was LeRoy's top key to success.

"Strangely...no," he said thinking it through. "As my mind raced to find a way to give you a future, I walked into the bank just two weeks before your first birthday and Jim said I had to come see him about this new company. He spent several hours with me, walking through the company and how buying stock worked. He reassured me of how he would be with me every step of the way. At that point, something on the inside of me said 'do it'; so I gave him $210 and bought 10 shares of Microsoft stock. I was scared out of my mind but looking back on it, *it was the best thing I ever did.*"

Grandbooty continued, "I have bought and traded with Jim ever since and I don't mind sharing with you that I make *more money* from my investments than I do from this farm. Me and Frankie have a secure living and I owe that to Jim and how he treated me when I didn't have nothin. Now we will leave a good legacy to our family. But don't get any ideas, I ain't going *nowhere* anytime soon!"

"You know I wouldn't have it any other way! Jim sounds like a good man," Matt asserted.

"He sure is. *I think you should meet him.* I don't know why I didn't think of that sooner! I have a standing lunch with him once a month. The next one is a week from tomorrow. I want you to join us. Jim won't mind as it will give him someone to talk to besides an old man. Maybe he knows something that can help you with your new job."

"I would love that. I have to tell you, I feel a little lost now that LeRoy is gone. *I know it is time to stand alone, but* how *do you know what to do when you feel pressure and are scared out of your mind?*"

"In a way, what I did with the stock was like these here eggs. Like Frankie said, 'all the other ingredients don't mean nothin without something to hold them together' -"

"A binding agent!" Matt declared.

"Right on! *In life, when something means more than life itself, you will find the courage to fight lions and faith to move mountains!*" he said energetically.

"That sounds like something LeRoy had tried to tell me. That if a man knows 'WHY' he wants a thing; he can bear almost any 'HOW'. He taught me that a sincere desire to accomplish your mission would take all the other ingredients and hold them together while the baking process was being completed. I have to tell you, I feel like I am in the oven right now," Matt admitted, knowing it was safe to expose his fears to his grandfather.

"You will do just fine. Remember, life is always teaching you...showing you the way with -"

"A trail of crumbs!!!" Matt exclaimed with a fresh revelation of how life would guide him.

"Exactly! Even with simple things like these here eggs there are lessons to be learned. <u>Desire is the tie that binds and gives you the gumption to follow your path</u>. Mr. LeRoy was right, when you want the answer *bad enough*, the answer will appear. The answer will also contain a resolve for you to do it!" he finished clinching his fist like an old-school prize fighter taking a swing in the air for dramatic effect.

At that moment, they walked into the kitchen, "You're right on time!" said Frankie to Grandbooty.

"Have I *ever* let you down?" he replied lovingly.

"*Never in 50 years*," she said with all the love of a 16 year old wearing his varsity jacket after the big game - belying their 50 plus years of marriage. She takes the eggs and hugs him and kisses him on the cheek.

The sweet scene was a reflection of how rich Grandbooty's life *truly was* - a richness that couldn't be measured in just money, alone. Moreover, Matt was comforted to know that Grandbooty could relate to his fears and that intense desire had motivated him to move beyond his natural comfort zones all those years ago. He made up his mind to always be on the lookout for the trail of crumbs - *the answers that would help him be successful.* Not just in his career, but in every area of his life, but for now, it was time to eat!

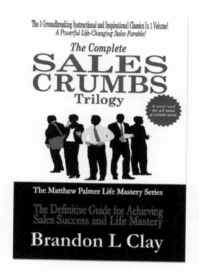

Continue the journey!!!

Purchase The Complete Sales Crumbs Trilogy at

www.brandonlclay.com

Amazon - hardcopy or kindle version

Apple I-store for I-Pads

All major online retailers!

About Brandon L. Clay

Brandon L. Clay is an author/story-teller, international speaker, and sales leader. For the past 28 years, he has delivered his distinctive brand of instruction and inspiration to over 30,000 sales professionals and 1,000's of others outside the sales arena. His strength is that he understands that there is no standardized template or "cookie cutter" approach to creating high sales achievers. His power of connection allows him to recognize and leverage each person's unique talents and help them unleash their greatest potential.

In February 2011, inspired by his father-in-law, LeRoy Shuffler, and combined with his experience of the 1,000's of people touched and transformed by his unique combination of life and sales mastery, he penned **Sales Crumbs from the Master's Table**. Brandon's entertaining, empowering, and enlightening approach to coaching sales excellence is brought to life through this simple story. It quickly become regarded as a *must read* for anyone in sales and inspired the follow-up volumes in the Trilogy - **A Trail of Sales Crumbs** and **Feasting On Sales Crumbs**. This trilogy is now touching everyone from CEO's, VP's, managers, seasoned veterans, to "newbies" in their first week and helping him fulfill his mission of Helping Millions Achieve Success...One At A Time.

ABOUT BRANDON L. CLAY

He lives in McDonough, Georgia with his high school sweetheart, Natalie, and their 3 children, Chaz, Christian, and Faith.

Learn more about Brandon, his available programs and additional resources at

www.brandonlclay.com

Additional Titles Available from Brandon L Clay;

Sales Crumbs Trilogy
Volume I - Sales Crumbs from the Master's Table
The Complete Sales Crumbs Trilogy

Your Authentic Sales Voice - *Discovering and unleashing your most natural gift for greater sales success!*

The Power to Change - *7 Day Life Transformation Guide*
$S=ME^2$- *Revolutionary Success Formula!*

The 80% Sales Solution - *Training program based on the popular Sales Crumbs Trilogy*

21005191R00085

Made in the USA
Charleston, SC
05 August 2013